Practice
Book

Mc
Graw
Hill

mheducation.com/prek-12

Send all inquiries to:
McGraw Hill
1325 Avenue of the Americas
New York, NY 10019

ISBN: 978-1-26-579426-2
MHID: 1-26-579426-X

Printed in the United States of America.

7 8 9 SMN 26 25 24 23

Contents

Contents

UNIT 1
Take a New Step

Week 1

Phonological Awareness:
Onset and Rime Blending................39
Phonemic Awareness: Phoneme Isolation 40
Phoneme Categorization...................... 41
Phonics: Initial/final /m/m.............................42
Handwriting.. 43
High-Frequency Words: *the*.........................44
Category Words: Feeling Words 45
Grammar: Nouns/Edit/Proofread................46–48
Take-Home Story 49–50

Week 2

Phonological Awareness: Identify Rhyme...........51
Phonemic Awareness: Phoneme Isolation 52
Phoneme Blending....................................53
Phonics: Initial/medial /a/a 54
Handwriting..55
High-Frequency Words: *we, can*...............56
Category Words: *Family Words*.....................57
Grammar: Nouns/Edit/Proofread...................58–60
Take-Home Story 61–62

Week 3

Phonological Awareness:
Onset/Rime Blending......................................63
Phonemic Awareness:
Phoneme Isolation 64
Phoneme Blending......................................65
Phonics: Initial /s/s.....................................66
Handwriting..67
High-Frequency Words: *see, the*...........68
Category Words: Sensory Words.................69
Grammar: Nouns/Edit/Proofread................... 70–72
Take-Home Story 73–74

UNIT 2
Let's Explore

Week 1

Phonological Awareness: Identify Alliteration......75
Phonemic Awareness:
Phoneme Isolation 76
Phoneme Blending 77
Phonics: Initial/final /p/p 78
Phonics/Spelling 79
Phonics: Letter/Sound Match 80
Handwriting.. 81
High-Frequency Words: *a, see*...............82
Category Words: Colors................................. 83
Grammar: Verbs/Edit/Proofread....................84–86
Take-Home Story 87–88

Week 2

Phonological Awareness:
Onset/Rime Blending.. 89
Phonemic Awareness: Phoneme Isolation 90
Phoneme Blending 91
Phonics: Initial/final /t/t 92
Phonics/Spelling 93
Phonics: Letter/Sound Match 94
Handwriting..95
High-Frequency Words: *like, a*...................96
Category Words: Shapes................................ 97
Grammar: Verbs/Edit/Proofread...................98–100
Take-Home Story 101–102

Week 3

Phonological Awareness:
Count and Segment Syllables 103
Phonics: Letter Review 104–105
Phonics/Spelling 106
High-Frequency Words Review............................ 107
Category Words: Textures 108
Category Words Review 109
Grammar: Verbs/Edit/Proofread....................110–112
Take-Home Story 113–114

Copyright © McGraw Hill. Permission is granted to reproduce for classroom use.

Name _____

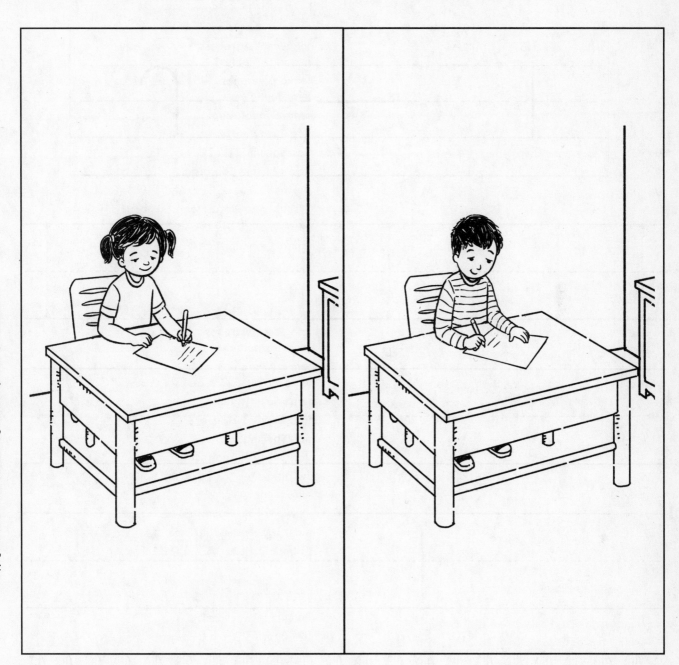

Handwriting

Model for children the correct way to sit up, hold a pencil, and have the correct paper placement. Say: *The picture on the left shows the way a left-handed person writes. The picture on the right shows the way a right-handed person writes.* Then tell children to sit up straight with their feet on the floor. Have them practice sitting up straight, holding a pencil, and slanting their paper.

Name _____

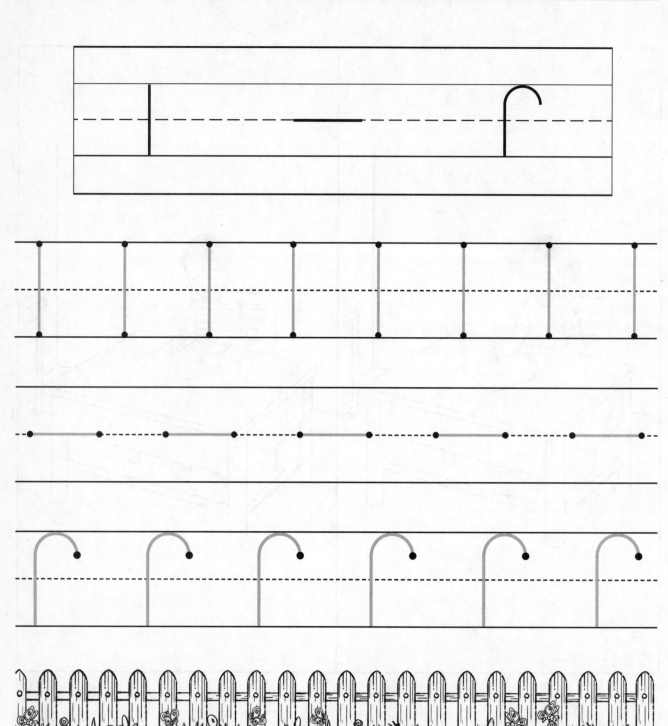

Letter Formation

Point to the first letter form at the top of the page. Explain to children that some letters are formed using a straight line that goes up and down. Point to the second letter form and tell children that other letters are formed with straight lines that go from left to right. Point to the third letter form and explain that still other letters are formed using a curved line and a straight line. Tell children to then trace the letter forms in each row.

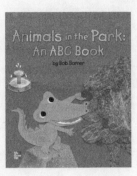  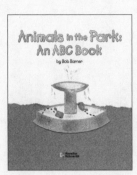

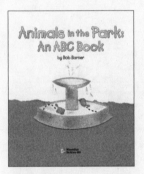 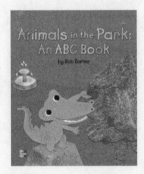 

 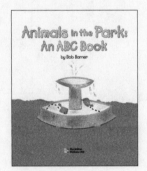 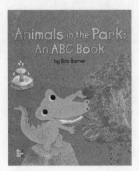

Concepts of Print

Show children the front cover, the back cover, and the title page of *Animals in the Park*. Explain what each one shows. Model these concepts of print. Then have children do the following:

🍎 Circle the picture that shows the back cover.

★ Circle the picture that shows the front cover.

🌲 Circle the picture that shows the title page.

Name _____

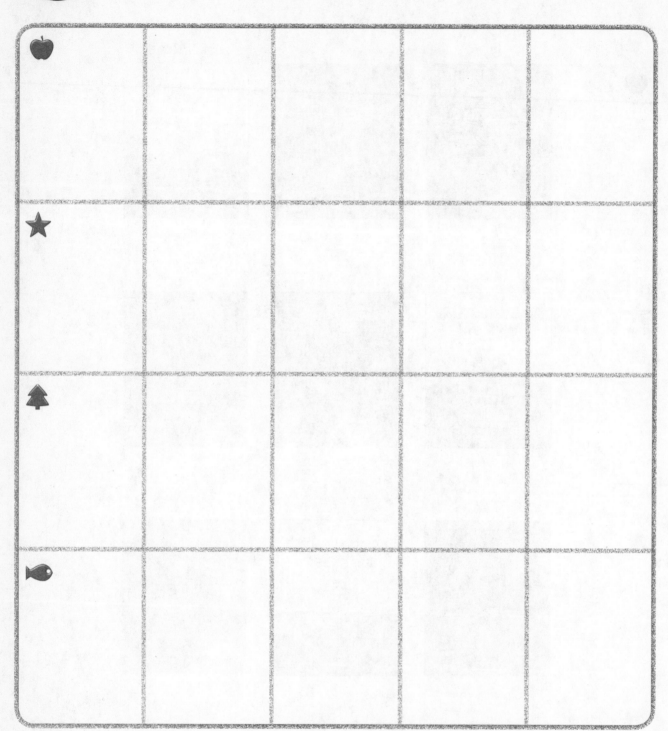

Phonological Awareness: Sentence Segmentation
Explain to children that sentences are made up of words. Say: *I like to learn.* Tell children that there are four words in the sentence. Hold up a finger for each word in the sentence. Tell children you will color in four boxes to show that there are four words in the sentence. Then tell children to color in a box for each word that they hear in the following sentences: ★ *It is sunny out.* ♣ *Please turn to page four.* ➤ *I can.* Then have children identify the words in each of the sentences.

4 Grade K • Start Smart • Week I

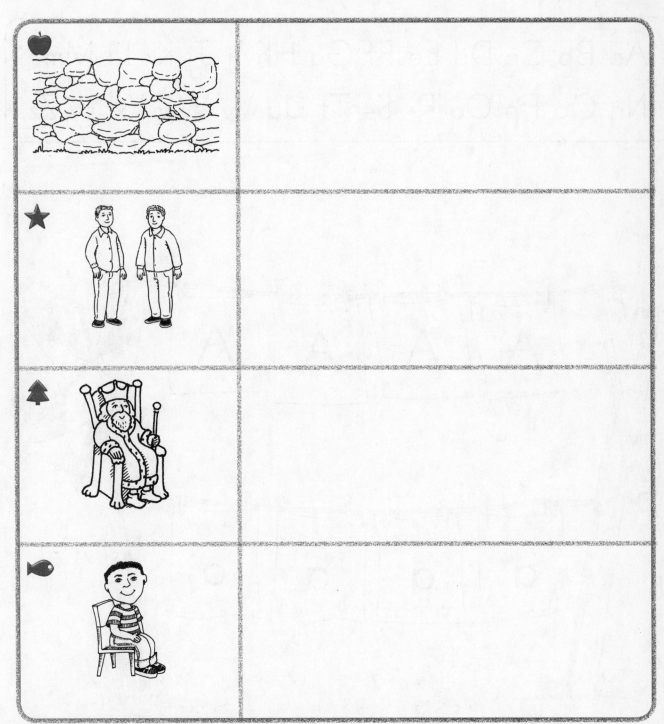

Phonological Awareness: Nursery Rhyme
Explain to children that a nursery rhyme is a short rhyme that tells a story. It also has a beat or rhythm. Tell children that you will read the nursery rhyme "Humpty Dumpty" aloud. Encourage them to listen as you clap to the beat. Say: *The beat that you hear is the rhythm.* Repeat the rhyme again, this time asking children to clap to the beat. Tell children to also listen for rhyming words, or words that end the same way as in *net* and *pet*. Draw a picture of something that rhymes with the picture of the wall in the first row and discuss with children. Then have them draw something that rhymes with the other picture names.

Name _____

Aa Bb Cc Dd Ee Ff Gg Hh Ii Jj Kk Ll Mm
Nn Oo Pp Qq Rr Ss Tt Uu Vv Ww Xx Yy Zz

Letter Recognition: *Aa*

Point to and say the uppercase and lowercase forms of the letter *Aa*. Tell children that the uppercase *A* is used if it's the first word in a sentence or the first letter in a person's name, such as *Amy*. Tell children to draw a line from each uppercase letter *A* to each lowercase *a* on the page.

Name _____

Aa Bb Cc Dd Ee Ff Gg Hh Ii Jj Kk Ll Mm
Nn Oo Pp Qq Rr Ss Tt Uu Vv Ww Xx Yy Zz

Letter Recognition: _Bb_
Point to and say the uppercase and lowercase forms of the letter _Bb_. Tell children that the uppercase _B_ is used if it's the first word in a sentence or the first letter in a person's name, such as _Bonnie_. Tell children to draw a line from each uppercase letter _B_ to each lowercase _b_ on the page.

Aa Bb Cc Dd Ee Ff Gg Hh Ii Jj Kk Ll Mm
Nn Oo Pp Qq Rr Ss Tt Uu Vv Ww Xx Yy Zz

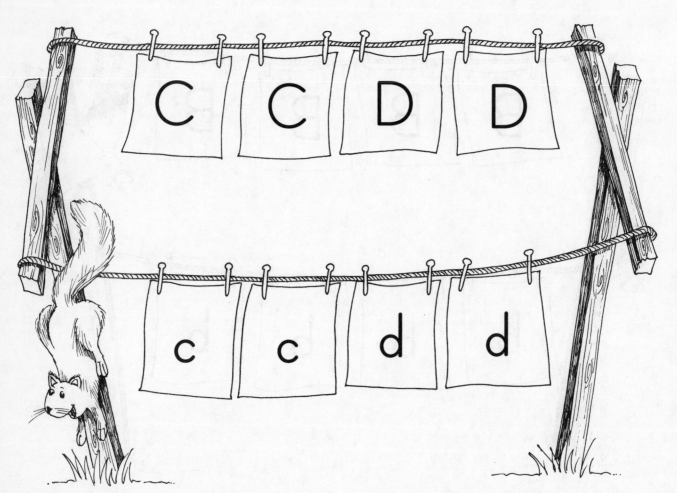

Letter Recognition: *Cc, Dd*
Point to and say the uppercase and lowercase forms of the letter *Cc*. Tell children that the uppercase *C* is used if it's the first word in a sentence or the first letter in a person's name, such as *Carol*. Tell children to draw a line from each uppercase *C* to each lowercase *c* on the page. Repeat with the uppercase and lowercase forms of the letter *Dd* and the name *Dan*.

Aa Bb Cc Dd Ee Ff Gg Hh Ii Jj Kk Ll Mm
Nn Oo Pp Qq Rr Ss Tt Uu Vv Ww Xx Yy Zz

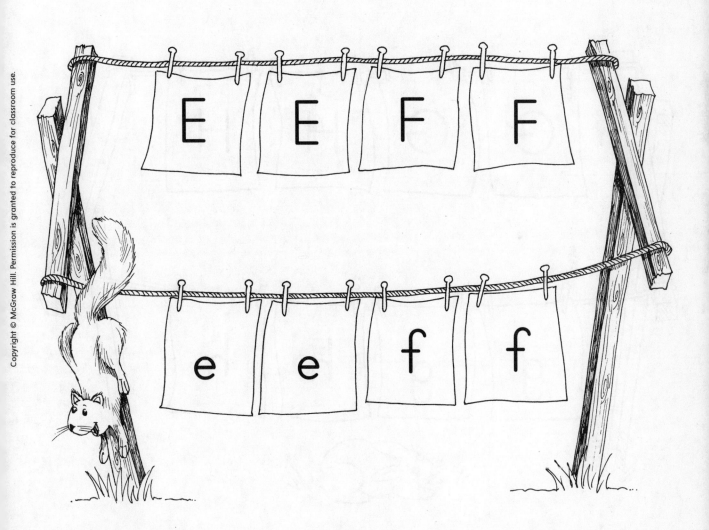

Letter Recognition: *Ee, Ff*
Point to and say the uppercase and lowercase forms of the letter *Ee*. Tell children that the uppercase *E* is used if it's the first word in a sentence or the first letter in a person's name, such as *Ed*. Tell children to draw a line from each uppercase letter *E* to each lowercase *e*. Repeat with the uppercase and lowercase forms of the letter *Ff* and the name *Finn*.

Name _____

Aa Bb Cc Dd Ee Ff Gg Hh Ii Jj Kk Ll Mm
Nn Oo Pp Qq Rr Ss Tt Uu Vv Ww Xx Yy Zz

Letter Recognition: *Gg, Hh*

Point to and say the uppercase and lowercase forms of the letter *Gg*. Tell children that the uppercase *G* is used if it's the first word in a sentence or the first letter in a person's name, such as *Gabe*. Tell children to draw a line from each uppercase letter *G* to each lowercase letter *g*. Repeat with the uppercase and lowercase forms of the letter *Hh* and the name *Hannah*.

Name _____

Category Words: Names

Explain to children that people have names to identify them, such as *Amy* and *Dave*. Tell children that some of the pictures on this page show children with names. Point to and name the pictures in each row. Have children circle the pictures that show names. Then have partners use the names in sentences.

Write

Name _____

_____

- - - - - - - - - - - - - -

_____

●

_____

- - - - - - - - - - - - - -

_____

●

_____

- - - - - - - - - - - - - -

_____

●

_____

- - - - - - - - - - - - - -

_____

●

High-Frequency Words: *I*

Model the Read/Spell/Write routine using the word *I*. Have children repeat the routine. Point to and say the names of the picture in each row. Then have children write the word *I* on the line to complete each sentence. Then say the word *I* for children to spell. Then have pairs of children read each sentence to a partner.

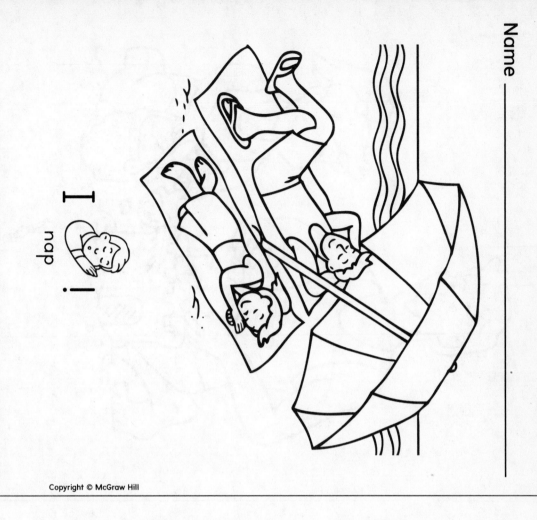

I

nap

Connect to Community
Encourage children to read the story to a family member or a friend.

Grade K • Start Smart • Week I

I hop

I hop

Review High-Frequency Words
Have children set a purpose for reading, such as finding out what the boy and girl can do. Explain that words in a sentence are separated by spaces. Model pointing to the space between words. Then ask children to point to the space between the word *I* and the rebus of the boy hopping on page I.

I dig.

3

I throw.

2

Name _____

Concepts of Print

Show children the front cover, the back cover, and the title page of *The Big Book of Rhymes*. Explain what each one shows. Model these concepts of print. Then have children do the following:

🍎 Circle the picture that shows the front cover.
★ Circle the picture that shows the title page.
🌲 Circle the picture that shows the back cover.

Name _____

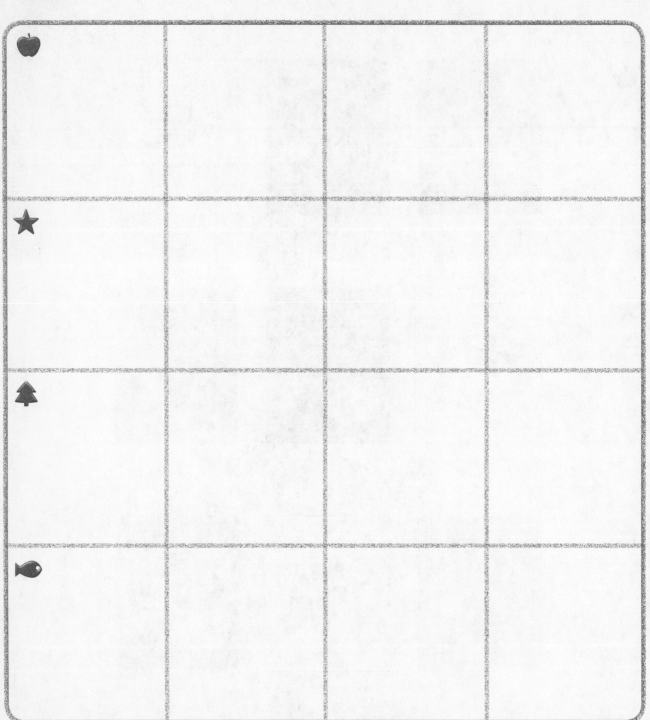

Phonological Awareness: Sentence Segmentation
Explain to children that sentences are made up of words. Say: *We raise our hands*. Tell children that there
are four words in the sentence. Hold up a finger for each word in the sentence. Tell children you will color
in four boxes to show that there are four words in the sentence. Then tell children to color in a box for each
word that they hear in the following sentences: ★ *I ate a sandwich.* ♠ *You can go.* ► *Can you help?* Then
have children identify the individual words in each sentence.

Name _____

Phonological Awareness: Nursery Rhyme
Explain to children that a nursery rhyme is a short rhyme that tells a story. Point out that a nursery rhyme has a beat or rhythm. Tell children that you will read the nursery rhyme "1, 2, 3, 4, 5" aloud. Clap to the beat as you read the rhyme. Repeat the rhyme, this time asking children to clap to the beat. Encourage children to listen for rhyming words, or words that end the same way as in *mat* and *pat*. Tell children to draw a picture of something that rhymes with the name of the picture in each row.

Grade K • Start Smart • Week 2 **17**

Name _____

Aa Bb Cc Dd Ee Ff Gg Hh Ii Jj Kk Ll Mm
Nn Oo Pp Qq Rr Ss Tt Uu Vv Ww Xx Yy Zz

Letter Recognition: Ii, Jj
Point to and say the uppercase and lowercase forms of the letter *Ii*. Tell children that the uppercase letter *I* is used if it's the first word in a sentence or the first letter in a person's name, such as *Ingrid*. Tell children to draw a line from each uppercase letter *I* to each lowercase *i*. Repeat with the uppercase and lowercase forms of the letter *Jj* and the name *Jack*.

Aa Bb Cc Dd Ee Ff Gg Hh Ii Jj Kk Ll Mm
Nn Oo Pp Qq Rr Ss Tt Uu Vv Ww Xx Yy Zz

Letter Recognition: *Kk, Ll*
Point to and say the uppercase and lowercase forms of the letter *Kk*. Tell children that the uppercase letter *K* is used if it's the first word in a sentence or the first letter in a person's name, such as *Ken*. Tell children to draw a line from each uppercase letter *K* to each lowercase *k*. Repeat with the uppercase and lowercase forms of the letter *Ll* and the name *Lee*.

Aa Bb Cc Dd Ee Ff Gg Hh Ii Jj Kk Ll Mm
Nn Oo Pp Qq Rr Ss Tt Uu Vv Ww Xx Yy Zz

Letter Recognition: *Mm, Nn*
Point to and say the uppercase and lowercase forms of the letter *Mm*. Tell children that the uppercase letter *M* is used if it's the first word in a sentence or the first letter in a person's name, such as *Meg*. Tell children to draw a line from each uppercase letter *M* to each lowercase *m*. Repeat with the uppercase and lowercase forms of the letter *Nn* and the name *Nan*.

Aa Bb Cc Dd Ee Ff Gg Hh Ii Jj Kk Ll Mm
Nn Oo Pp Qq Rr Ss Tt Uu Vv Ww Xx Yy Zz

Letter Recognition: *Oo, Pp*
Point to and say the uppercase and lowercase forms of the letter *Oo*. Tell children that the uppercase letter *O* is used if it's the first word in a sentence or the first letter in a person's name, such as *Olivia*. Tell children to draw a line from each uppercase letter *O* to each lowercase *o*. Repeat with the uppercase and lowercase forms of the letter *Pp* and the name *Pam*.

Aa Bb Cc Dd Ee Ff Gg Hh Ii Jj Kk Ll Mm
Nn Oo Pp Qq Rr Ss Tt Uu Vv Ww Xx Yy Zz

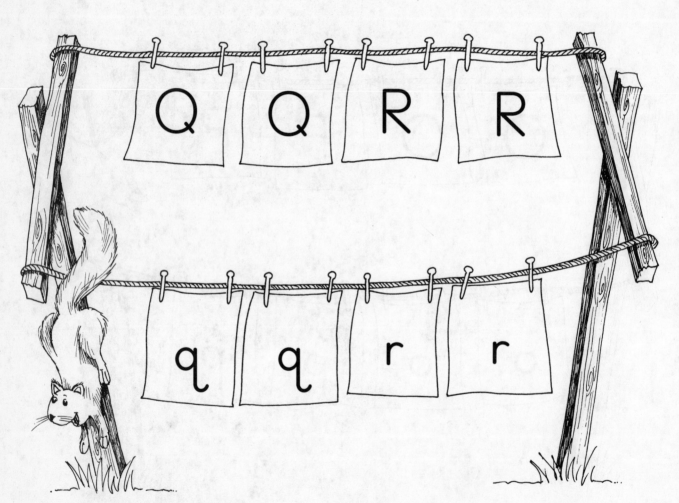

Letter Recognition: *Qq, Rr*
Point to and say the uppercase and lowercase forms of the letter *Qq*. Tell children that the uppercase letter *Q* is used if it's the first word in a sentence or the first letter in a person's name, such as *Quinn*. Tell children to draw a line from each uppercase letter *Q* to each lowercase *q*. Repeat with the uppercase and lowercase forms of the letter *Rr* and the name *Robert*.

5   D   10

2   4   a

L   3   7

Category Words: Numbers
Explain to children that they will be learning numbers in addition to letters. Say: *A number tells how many there are of something.* Say: *Ten is a number. There are 10 children in the library.* Tell children that some of the pictures on this page show numbers. Point to and name the numbers and letters in each row. Have children circle the pictures that show numbers.

Name _____

🍎 I _____
     - - - - - - - - - - - - - - - - - - -
     _____

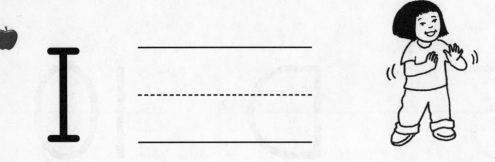

                                                          ●

⭐ I _____
     - - - - - - - - - - - - - - - - - - -
     _____

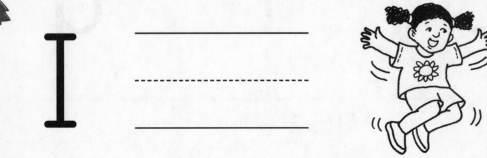

                                                          ●

🌲 I _____
     - - - - - - - - - - - - - - - - - - -
     _____

                                                           ●

🐟 I _____
     - - - - - - - - - - - - - - - - - - -
     _____

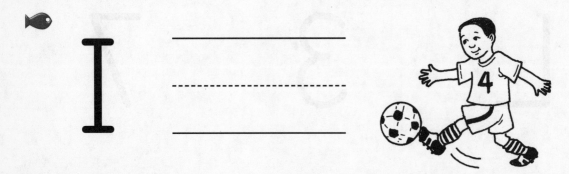

                                                           ●

High-Frequency Words
Model the Read/Spell/Write routine using the word *can*. Have children repeat the routine. Point to and say the names of the picture in each row. Then have children write the word *can* on the line to complete each sentence. Say the words *I* and *can* for children to spell. Encourage pairs of children to tell each other what they can do.

Name _____

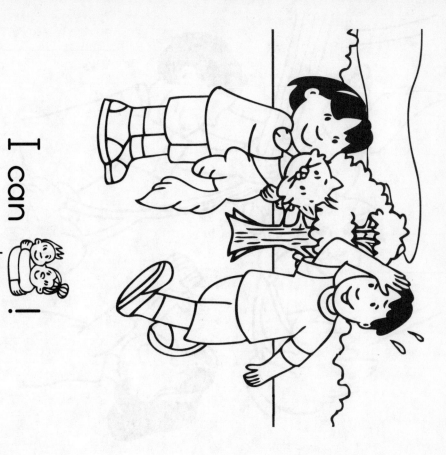

I can
hug
!

Connect to Community
Encourage children to read the story to a family member or a friend.

I Can
hug
!

I can
see
!

Review High-Frequency Words
Have children set a purpose for reading, such as finding out what the girl can do. Explain that words in a sentence are separated by spaces. Model pointing to the space between the words *I* and *can* on page 1. Then tell children to point to the space between the words *I* and *can* on page 4.

I can  catch .

I can  yell .

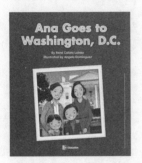

Concepts of Print

Show children the front cover, the back cover, and the title page of *Ana Goes to Washington*. Explain what each one shows. Model these concepts of print. Then have children do the following:

- Circle the picture that shows the front cover.
- Circle the picture that shows the title page.
- Circle the picture that shows the back cover.

Grade K • Start Smart • Week 3 **27**

Phonological Awareness: Recognize Syllables
Point to the apple and say its name. Model clapping for each syllable or part in the word. Point out that
there are two parts or syllables in *apple*. Tell children that you will write the number 2 in the box because
apple has two parts or syllables. Point to and name the picture in each row. Tell children to write a number
on the line to show how many parts or syllables they hear. Then have children identify the parts or syllables
in each word.

Name _____

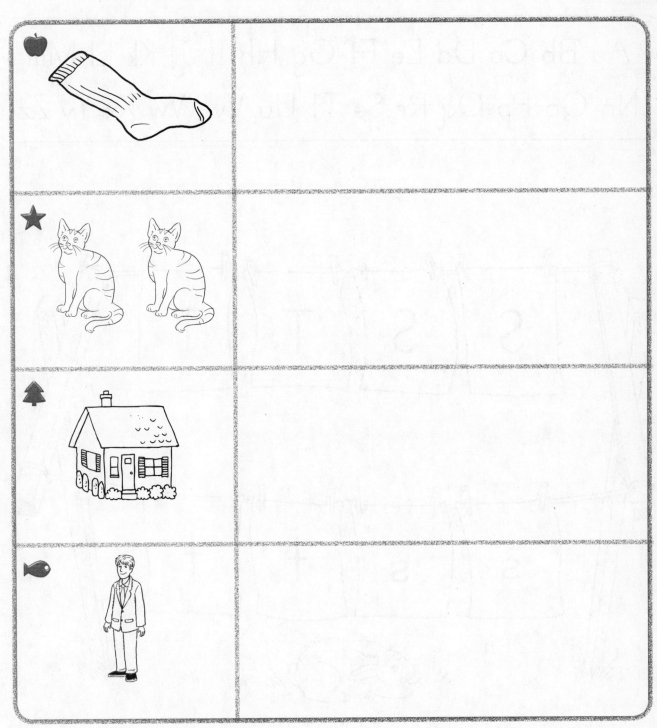

Phonological Awareness: Nursery Rhyme

Explain to children that a nursery rhyme is a short rhyme that tells a story. Tell children that you will read the nursery rhyme "As I Was Going to St. Ives" aloud. Encourage them to listen for rhyming words, or words that end the same way as in *vet* and *get*. Explain to children that nursery rhymes have a beat or rhythm. As you read the rhyme, emphasize the beat by clapping. Tell children to draw a picture of something that rhymes with the name of the picture in each row.

Name _____

Aa Bb Cc Dd Ee Ff Gg Hh Ii Jj Kk Ll Mm
Nn Oo Pp Qq Rr Ss Tt Uu Vv Ww Xx Yy Zz

Letter Recognition: *Ss, Tt*
Point to and say the uppercase and lowercase forms of the letter *Ss*. Tell children that the uppercase *S* is used if it's the first word in a sentence or the first letter in a person's name, such as *Sam*. Tell children to draw a line from the uppercase *S* to the lowercase *s* on the page. Repeat with the uppercase and lowercase letters *Tt* and the name *Tam*.

Name _____

Aa Bb Cc Dd Ee Ff Gg Hh Ii Jj Kk Ll Mm
Nn Oo Pp Qq Rr Ss Tt Uu Vv Ww Xx Yy Zz

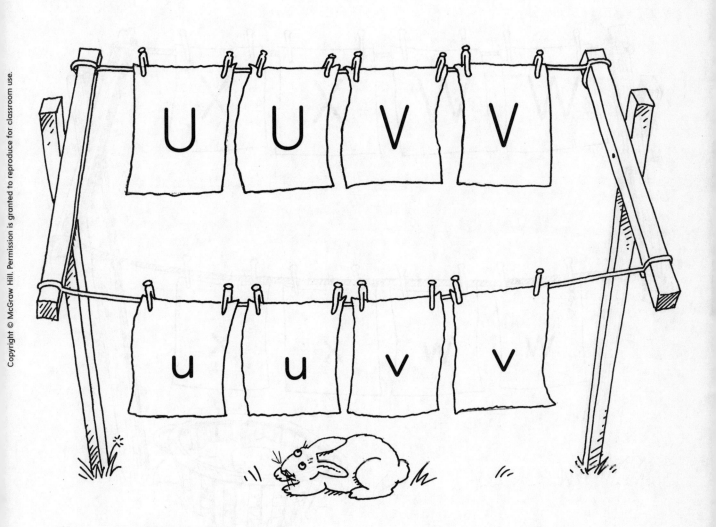

Letter Recognition: *Uu, Vv*
Point to and say the uppercase and lowercase forms of the letter *Uu*. Tell children that the uppercase *U* is used if it's the first word in a sentence or the first letter in a person's name, such as *Uma*. Tell children to draw a line from the uppercase *U* to the lowercase *u* on the page. Repeat with the uppercase and lowercase letter *Vv* and the name *Vicky*.

Name _____

Aa Bb Cc Dd Ee Ff Gg Hh Ii Jj Kk Ll Mm
Nn Oo Pp Qq Rr Ss Tt Uu Vv Ww Xx Yy Zz

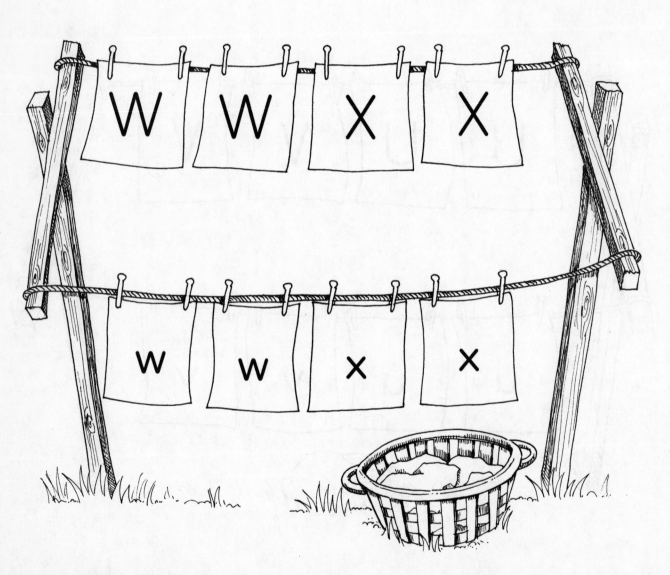

Letter Recognition: Ww, Xx
Point to and say the uppercase and lowercase forms of the letter Ww. Tell children that the uppercase letter W is used if it's the first word in a sentence or the first letter in a person's name, such as Wendy. Tell children to draw a line from each uppercase letter W to each lowercase w. Repeat with the uppercase and lowercase forms of the letter Xx and the name Xing.

Aa Bb Cc Dd Ee Ff Gg Hh Ii Jj Kk Ll Mm
Nn Oo Pp Qq Rr Ss Tt Uu Vv Ww Xx Yy Zz

Letter Recognition: *Yy, Zz*

Point to and say the uppercase and lowercase forms of the letter *Yy*. Tell children that the capital letter *Y* is used if it's the first word in a sentence or the first letter in a person's name, such as *Yolanda*. Tell children to draw a line from each uppercase letter *Y* to each lowercase *y*. Repeat with the uppercase and lowercase forms of the letter *Zz* and the name *Zachary*. Then direct children's attention to the alphabet at the top of the page and say the name of each uppercase and lowercase letter. Then name random uppercase and lowercase letters and have children identify them.

Name _____

Aa Bb Cc Dd Ee Ff Gg Hh Ii Jj Kk Ll Mm
Nn Oo Pp Qq Rr Ss Tt Uu Vv Ww Xx Yy Zz

🍎   F   g   e   f   x

⭐   M   z   E   n   m

🌲   Q   o   q   b   c

🐟   S   t   c   o   s

Letter Identification Review
Review the alphabet with children. Then tell them to look at the uppercase letter in each row.
Have children follow these directions:

🍎 Circle the lowercase *f*.   ⭐ Circle the lowercase *m*.
🌲 Circle the lowercase *q*.   🐟 Circle the lowercase *s*.

Have children take turns working with partners to identify the letters on the chart at the top of this page.
Then guide children to turn to The Alphabet page on page 463. Have them identify all the uppercase
letters, and then all the lowercase letters.

34   Grade K • Start Smart • Week 3

Name _____

3

a b c d e f
g h i j k l m
n o p q r s
t u v w x y z

can

Category Words: Days of the Week
Explain to children that there are seven days of the week. Name the days: *Sunday, Monday, Tuesday, Wednesday, Thursday, Friday* and *Saturday*. Ask children how the days *Saturday* and *Sunday* are different from the other days of the week. Tell children that some of the pictures on this page show days of the week. Point to and name the pictures in each row. Have children circle the pictures that show days of the week. Have partners talk about what they do on Saturday and Sunday.

Name _____

I   can

 _____

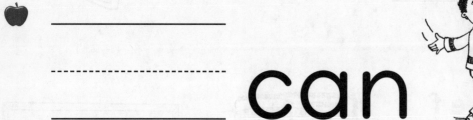  •

I _____
------------------------------  •

I _____
------------------------------  •

High-Frequency Words
Model the Read/Spell/Write routine with the words *I* and *can*. Have children choose a word from the box to complete each sentence. Have partners read the sentences to each other and talk about which of the things they can do on the page. Then say the words *I* and *can* for children to spell.

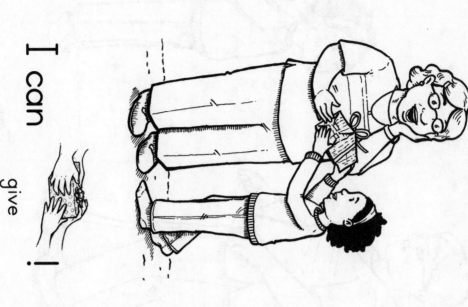

I can
give .

Connect to Community
Encourage children to read the story to a family member or a friend.

I Can

Give .

I can
cut .

Review High-Frequency Words
Have children set a purpose for reading, such as finding out what the girl can do. Explain that words in a sentence are separated by spaces. Model pointing to the space between the words *I* and *can* on page 1. Then ask children to point to the space between the words *I* and *can* on page 3.

1

I can ___ .

hide

I can ___ .

tie

Name _____

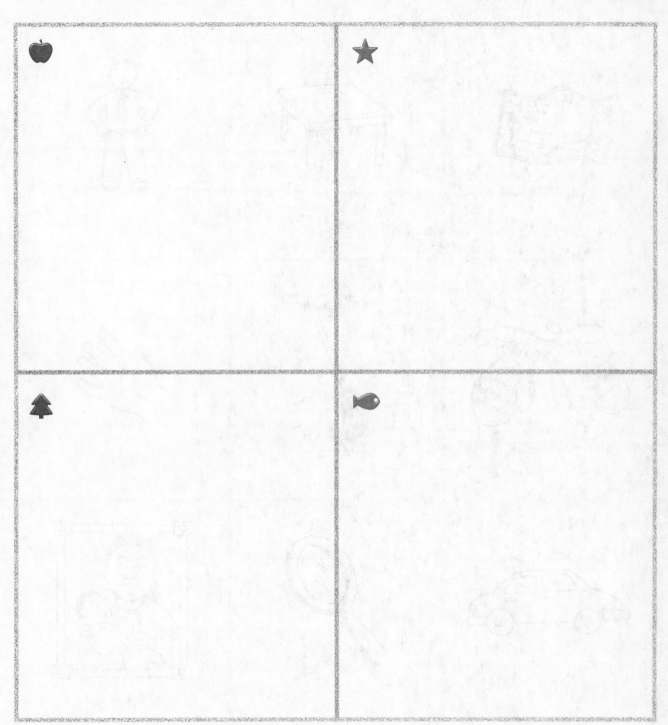

Phonological Awareness: Onset and Rime Blending
Explain to children that words have beginning and ending sounds. Listen as I say a word in parts, and then blend the word. Say /m/ /ap/, /maaap/, map. Have children repeat. Tell children you will draw a map in the first box. Then say the onset and rime of the following words. Have children blend the sounds to say the word. Then have them draw a picture in each box to show the word. ★ /b/ /ôl/, 🌲 /h/ /at/, 🐟 /b/ /ug/.

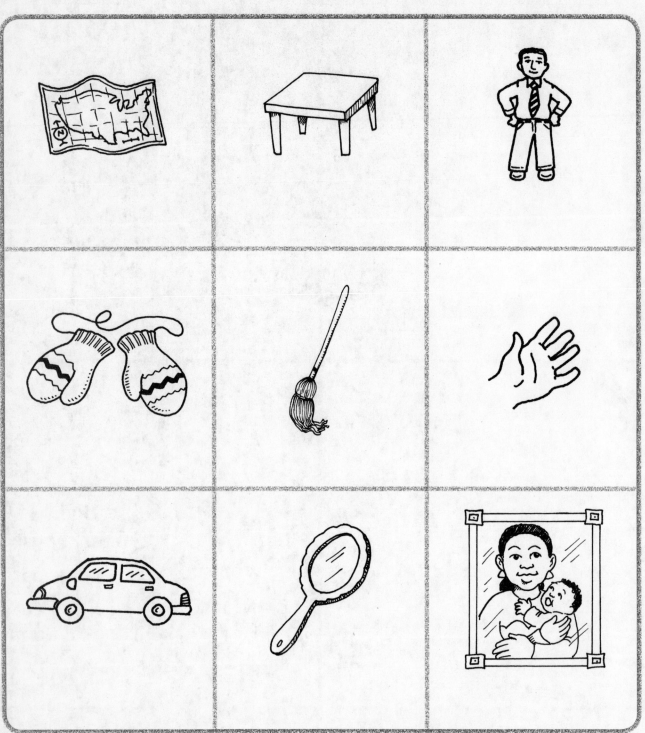

Phonemic Awareness: Phoneme Categorization

Point to and say the name of the pictures in each row. Tell children to circle the two pictures in each row that begin with the /m/ sound as in mix. Have children make an X on the picture that does not begin with /m/.

Name _____

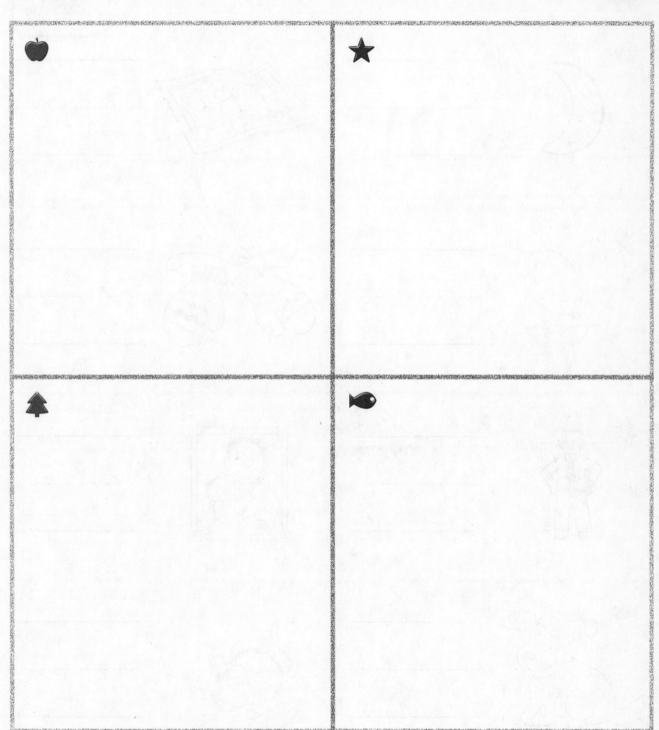

Phonemic Awareness: Phoneme Blending with /m/
Tell children to listen to the sounds in the word *mat*. Model blending the sounds to say the word *mat*, /mmmaaat/, *mat*. Have children repeat. Then tell children you will draw a picture of a mat in the first box. Then say the sounds in more words. Have them blend the sounds to say each word. Then have them draw a picture of the word: ★ /m//a//n/; 🌲 /p//a//d/; 🐟 /m//a//p/.

🍎 _____ _____

m

_____ _____

⭐ _____ _____

_____ _____

🌲 _____ _____

_____ _____

🐟 _____ _____

_____ _____

Phonics: /m/ m

Point to and say the name of the picture of the moon. Tell children that the word *moon* begins with the /m/ sound. Explain that the letter *m* stands for the /m/ sound. Now point to and say the names of the rest of the pictures on the page. Have children write the letter *m* next to the picture if its name begins with /m/ sound as in *moon*. Tell children to look at the pictures in each row from left to right.

Name _____

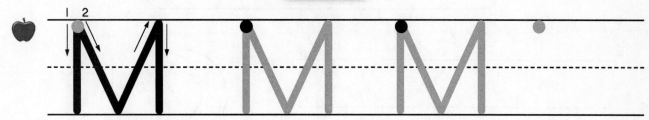

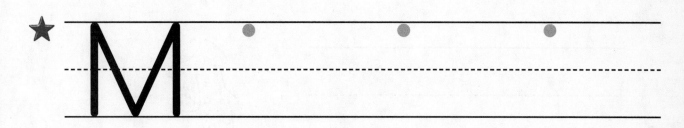

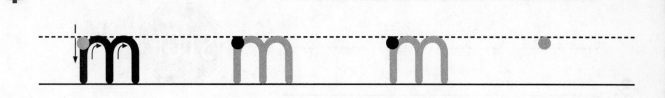

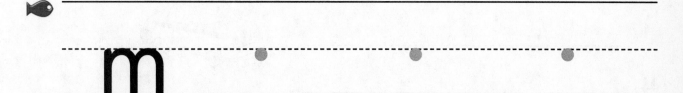

Handwriting: *Mm*
Demonstrate following the numbers and arrows to model for children the proper formation of the capital
and lowercase *Mm.* To form the uppercase letter *M,* say: *Straight down. Go back to the top. Slant down.*
Slant up. Straight down. For the lowercase *m,* say: *Straight down. Around and straight down. Around and*
straight down. Have children use their finger to trace the models for the letter. Then have them write the
uppercase and lowercase forms of the letter *Mm.*

the

1. _____

2. _____

3. _____

4. _____

High-Frequency Word: *the*

Model the Read/Spell/Write routine using the word *the*. Have children repeat. Point to and name the pictures. Then tell children to write the word *the* on each line and say the picture name. Have partners read the phrases. Then dictate the word *the* and have children spell and write the word.

Name _____

Category Words: Feeling Words
Explain that the words *happy, sad,* and *excited* describe feelings. Then name the pictures in each row.
Have children circle the two pictures in each row that show feelings. Encourage children to use feeling
words in sentences with a partner.

Grade K • Unit I • Week I **45**

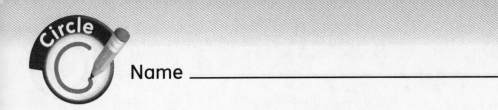

Name _____

person   place   animal   thing

The library is big.

The bird can fly.

The boy runs.

The fish swims.

Grammar: Singular Nouns
Point to and say the name of each picture at the top of the page. Explain to children that a noun is a word that names a person, place, animal, or thing. Tell children that *girl* is a noun that names a person; *library* is a noun that names a place or a location; *dog* is a noun that names an animal; *bike* is a noun that names a thing. Tell children to listen to each sentence. Have them circle the noun in each one and tell whether the noun names a person, a place, an animal, or a thing. Then encourage children to use nouns that name a person, a place, an animal, or a thing in sentences.

46 Grade K • Unit I • Week I

Name _____

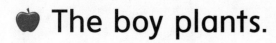

★ This store is new.

🌲 The nest is empty.

🐟 The wave is big.

Grammar: Singular Nouns

Remind children that a noun is a word that names a person, a place, an animal, or a thing. Remind children that some kinds of nouns name one person, place, animal, or thing. Say: *A girl names a person; the market names a place or location, a cat names an animal, and a ball names a thing.* Point to and say the names of the pictures on the page. Tell children to listen to each sentence, circle the noun and tell if it names one person, place, animal, or thing. Then tell children to refer back to a piece of writing that they did during the week and make sure they used nouns that name one person, place, animal or thing correctly.

🍎 i can see.

_____

- -

_____

★ The man sees

_____

- -

_____

🌲 the map is big.

_____

- -

_____

🐟 Can you pat the dog.

_____

- -

_____

Edit/Proofread
Read aloud the sentences. Tell children that a sentence begins with a capital letter and has an ending mark. Have children rewrite each sentence so it shows correct capitalization and end punctuation. Use gestures to clarify meaning when possible.

the
friends

Grade K · Unit 1 · Week 1

Connect to Community
Encourage children to read the story to a family member or a friend.

High-Frequency Word: the
Have children set a purpose for reading, such as finding out about the friends. Then explain that a word is made up of letters. Say: *The word the is made up of three letters, t, h, and e.* Ask children to point to the word *the* on page 2, and then to a letter in the word.

The
Friends

the
girl

1

the  dog

the boy

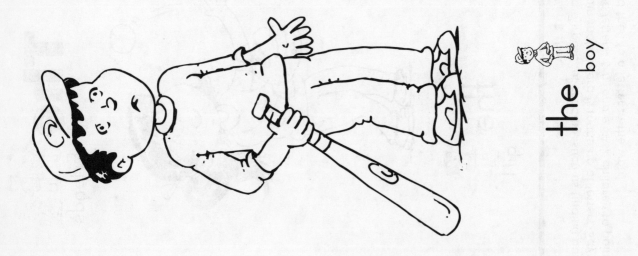

Name _____

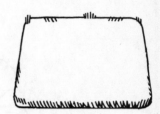

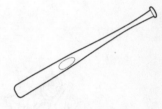

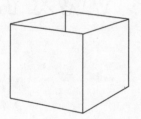

Phonological Awareness: Identify Rhyme
Explain to children that words that rhyme have the same ending sounds. Point to and name the pictures in the first row: *man, can, mat.* Say: *The words* man *and* can *rhyme because they have the same ending sounds.* They end with the sounds /an/. Tell children you will circle these pictures. Now point to and say the names of the other pictures on the page. Have children circle the two pictures in each row that have names that rhyme.

Name _____

Phonemic Awareness: /a/
Point to and say the name of the picture of the ant. Tell children that the word *ant* begins with the /a/ sound. Have children repeat, *ant*, /a/. Now point to and say the names of the rest of the pictures on the page. Tell children to circle the pictures that have names that begin with the /a/ sound as in *ant*.

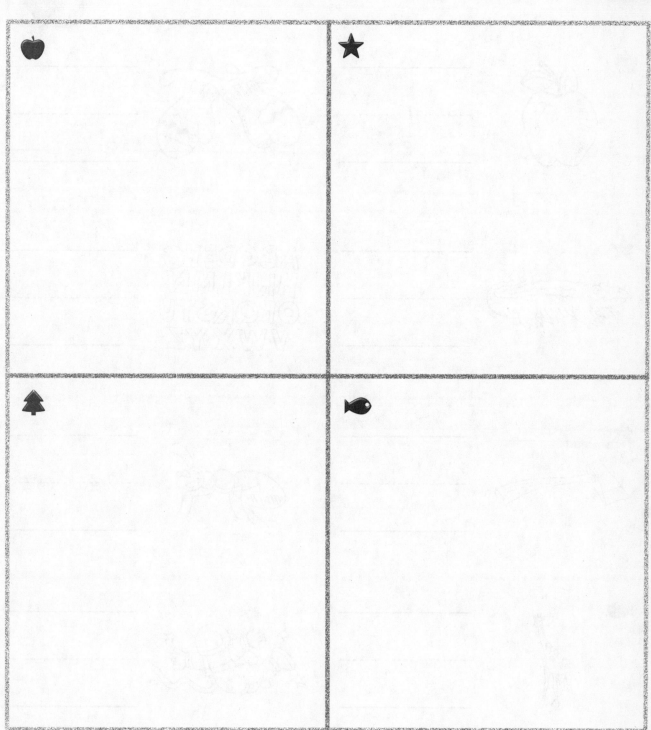

Phonemic Awareness: Phoneme Blending with /a/
Tell children to listen to the sounds in the word *at*. Model blending the sounds to say the word *at*, /aaat/, *at*. Point out your mouth position for each sound. Have children repeat. Then tell children you will say the sounds in more words. Have them blend the sounds to say each word. Then have them draw a picture of the word: /m//a//n/; /c//a//t/; /k//a//p/; /d//a//d/.

Grade K • Unit I • Week 2 **53**

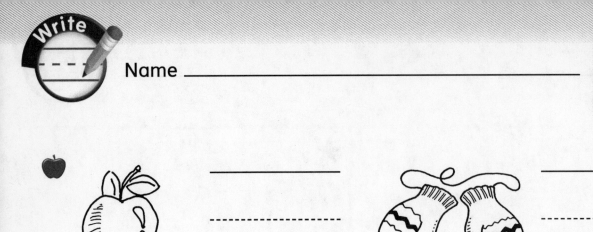
Name _____

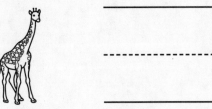

Phonics: /a/ a

Point to and say the name of the picture of the apple. Tell children that the word *apple* begins with the /a/ sound. Explain that the letter *a* stands for the /a/ sound. Now point to and say the names of the rest of the pictures on the page. Have children write the letter *a* next to the picture if its name begins with the /a/ sound as in *apple*. Tell children to look at the pictures in each row from left to right. Then tell them to work their way from the top of the page to the bottom.

Name _____

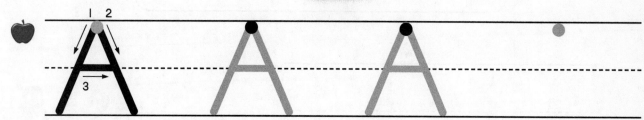

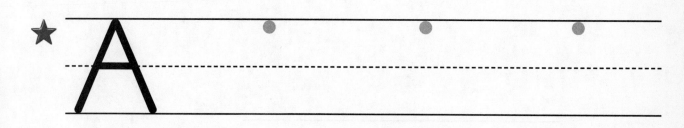

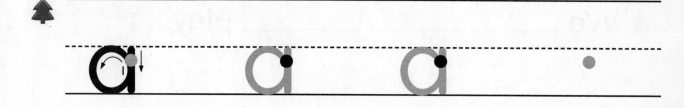

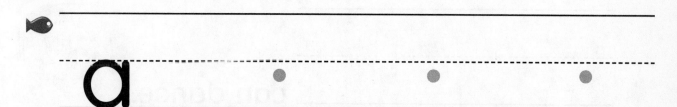

Handwriting: *Aa*

Demonstrate following the numbers and arrows to model the proper formation of the uppercase and lowercase *Aa*. To form the uppercase letter *A* say: *Slant down. Go back to the top. Slant down. Straight across the dotted line.* To form the lowercase letter *a* say: *Circle back, then around. Straight down.* Have children use their finger to trace the models for the letters. Then have them write the uppercase and lowercase forms of the letters *Aa*.

we · can

_____

- -

🍎 _____ can build.

_____

- -

⭐ We _____ play.

_____

- -

🌲 _____ can dance.

High-Frequency Words: *we, can*
Model the Read/Spell/Write routine with the word *we*. Have children repeat. Remind them that the other word in the box is *can*. Have children then write a word from the box on a line to complete each sentence. Have partners read the sentences to each other. Then dictate the words *we* and *can* for children to spell.

Name _____

Category Words: Family Words
Explain to children that different people make up a family. Then point to and name the pictures in each row. Have children circle the two pictures in each row that show who could belong in a family.

Name _____

cat　　bus　　cheese

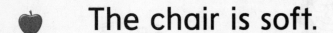 The chair is soft.

★ The egg is white.

🌲 The kite flies high.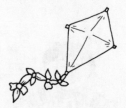

🐟 A grape is sweet.

Grammar: Singular Nouns
Remind children that a noun names a person, place, animal, or thing. Point to and name the pictures at the top of the page. Tell children that these are pictures of nouns that name one animal or thing. Then read each sentence and say the names of the pictures. Tell children to circle the noun in each sentence. Then tell children to refer back to a piece of writing that they did during the week and make sure they used nouns that name one animal or thing correctly.

_____

🍎 **I pet the** _____.

dog   big

_____

⭐ **My** _____ **is nice.**

ran   mom

_____

🌲 **The** _____ **is tall.**

tree   like

_____

🐟 **The** _____ **is pretty.**

jumps   girl

Grammar: Nouns
Read the sentences and word choices. Point to and say the name of each picture. Then tell children to write the word that completes each sentence on the lines. Use gestures to clarify meaning.

Name _____

🍎 i see it.

_____

_____

⭐ Can I sit.

_____

_____

🌲 I can nap

_____

_____

🐟 We can go?

_____

_____

Edit/Proofread

Tell children to listen as you read aloud the sentences. Have them rewrite each sentence so it shows correct capitalization and punctuation. Use gestures to clarify meaning.

We can

dig .

Connect to Community
Encourage children to read the story to a family member or a friend.

We Can!

We can

hop .

High-Frequency Words: we
Have children set a purpose for reading, such as finding out about what the different animals do. Explain that each word in a sentence is separated from the next word by a space. Point to the space between the words *We* and *can* on page 1. Then ask children to point to the space between the words *we* and *can* on page 3 of the story.

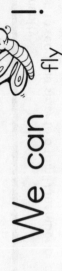

We can fly !

We can run .

Name _____

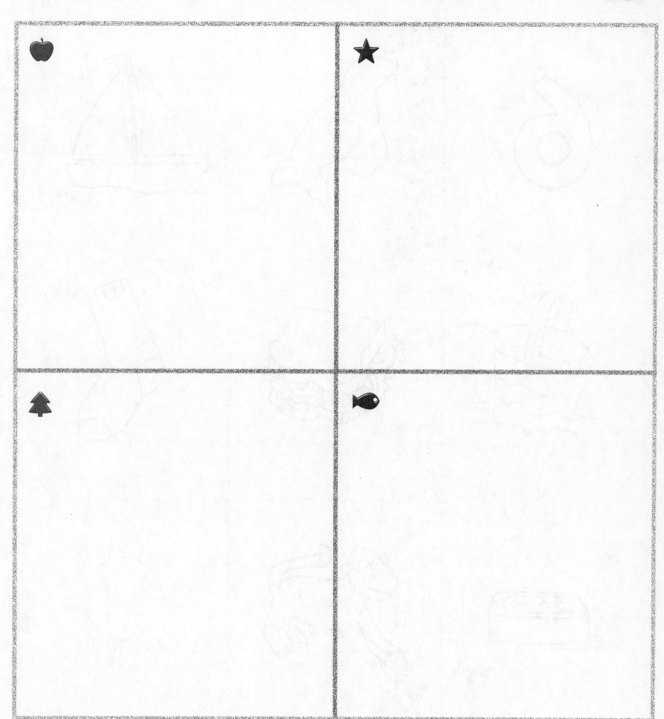

Phonological Awareness: Onset and Rime Blending

Explain to children that words are made up of beginning and ending sounds. Say the word *sit*. Now say /s/ followed by /it/. Blend the sounds to say *sit*. Have children repeat, /s/ /it/, /sit/, *sit*. Tell children that you will draw a picture of a person sitting in the first box. Then say the beginning and ending sounds in some other words. Tell children to blend the sounds to say the word. Have children draw a picture in each box that shows the picture name. ★ /s//ad/, *sad* 🌲 /m//at/, *mat* 🐟 /s//un/, *sun*.

Circle

Name _____

Phonemic Awareness: /s/

Point to and say the name of the picture of the number six. Tell children that the word *six* begins with the /s/ sound. Have children repeat, *six*, /s/. Now point to and say the names of the rest of the pictures on the page. Tell children to circle the pictures that have names that begin with the /s/ sound as in *six*.

64 Grade K • Unit I • Week 3

Name _____

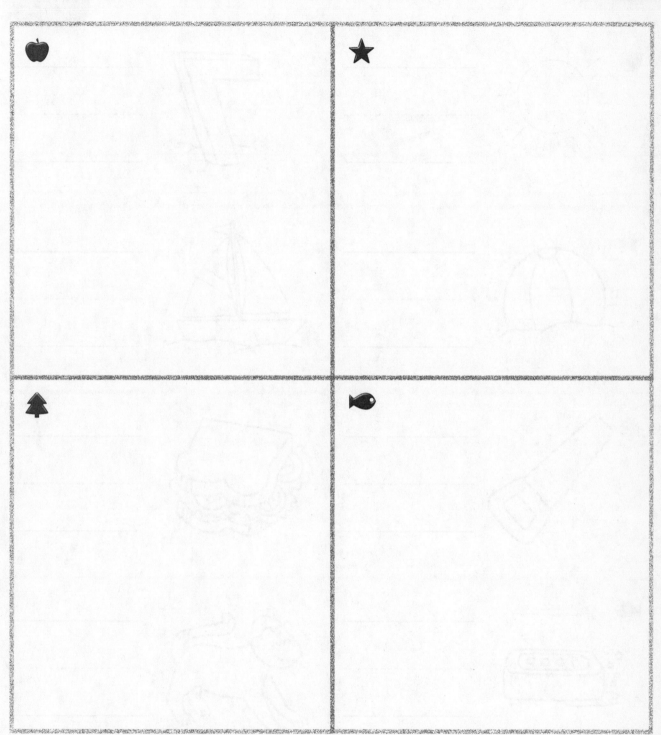

Phonemic Awareness: Phoneme Blending with /s/
Tell children to listen to the sounds in the word *sit*. Model blending the sounds to say the word *sit*, /sssiiit/, *sit*. Have children repeat. Then tell children you will say the sounds in more words. Have them blend the sounds to say each word. Then have them draw a picture of the word: /s//a//d/; /s//u//n/; /s//i//p/; /s//a//m/.

Grade K • Unit I • Week 3 **65**

 **Name** _____

 **Ss**

 _____
s _____

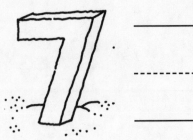 _____
_____

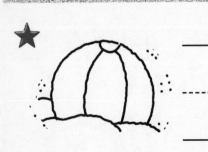 _____
_____

 _____
_____

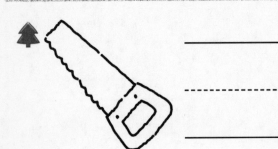 _____
_____

 _____
_____

 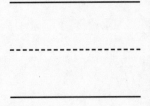 _____
_____

 _____
_____

Phonics: /s/s

Point to and say the word *sun* in the apple row. Say that it begins with the /s/ sound. Explain that the letter *s* stands for the /s/ sound. Now point to and say the name of each picture. Have children write the letter *s* next to the picture if its name begins with the /s/ sound as in *sun*. Remind children to look at the pictures in each row from left to right and to work their way from the top to the bottom of the page.

66 Grade K • Unit 1 • Week 3

Name _____

Ss

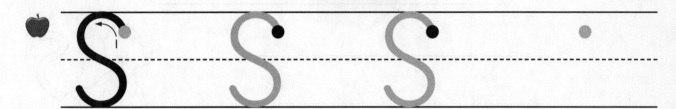

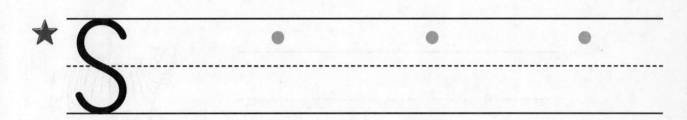

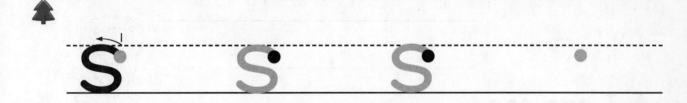

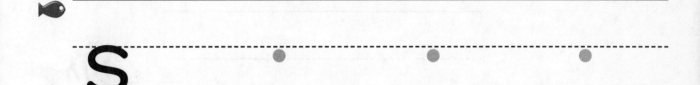

Handwriting: *Ss*

Demonstrate following the numbers and arrows to model for children the proper formation of the uppercase and lowercase letters *Ss*. To form the uppercase letter *S* say: *Circle back, sweep around, and back again.* To form the lowercase letter *s* say: *Circle back, then around. Straight down.* Have children use their finger to trace the models for the letters. Then have them write the uppercase and lowercase forms of the letters *Ss*.

Name _____

see	the

_____

- - - - - - - - - - - - - - - - - - -

🍎 We _____ the _____ .

_____

- - - - - - - - - - - - - - - - - - -

★ We _____ the _____ .

_____

- - - - - - - - - - - - - - - - - - -

🌲 I can see _____ .

_____

- - - - - - - - - - - - - - - - - - -

🐟 I can see _____ .

High-Frequency Words: *see, the*
Model the Read/Spell/Write routine with the word *see*. Have children repeat. Remind them that the other word is *the*. Tell children to repeat. Have them write a word from the box on the line to complete each sentence. Have partners read the sentences to each other. Then dictate *see* and *the* for children to spell.

Name _____

Category Words: Sensory Words
Explain that people use their senses to experience things. Say that **there** are five senses. Say that seeing, hearing, smelling, tasting, and touching are all senses. Point **to** and **name** the pictures in each row. Discuss how people are using their senses. Have children circle the **two-pictures** in each row that show people using their senses.

Name _____

home

classroom

town

🍎 The store is open.

⭐ The library is quiet.

🌲 The field is big.

🐟 The beach is hot.

Grammar: Nouns
Remind children that a noun names a person, a place, or a thing. Point to and name the pictures at the top of the page. Explain that these are all nouns that name places. Then read each sentence and point to and name the picture. Tell children to circle the noun in each sentence.

Name _____

_____

_____- -_____

🍎 My _____ grows.

house   plant

_____

- -

⭐ The _____ is warm.

pool   mitten

_____

- -

🌲 The _____ sails.

water   boat

_____

- -

🐟 The _____ helps animals.

table   vet

Grammar: Nouns
Remind children that a noun names a person, a place, or a thing. Then read each sentence and the two
answer choices. Point to and name the pictures. Tell children to write the noun that best completes each
sentence on the line.

🍎 You and i can hop.

_____

- -

_____

★ Can I sit.

_____

- -

_____

🌲 i sat with Sam.

_____

- -

_____

🐟 we can walk to school.

_____

- -

_____

Edit/Proofread
Tell children to listen as you read aloud the sentences. Have them rewrite each sentence so it shows
correct capitalization and punctuation. Use gestures to clarify meaning.

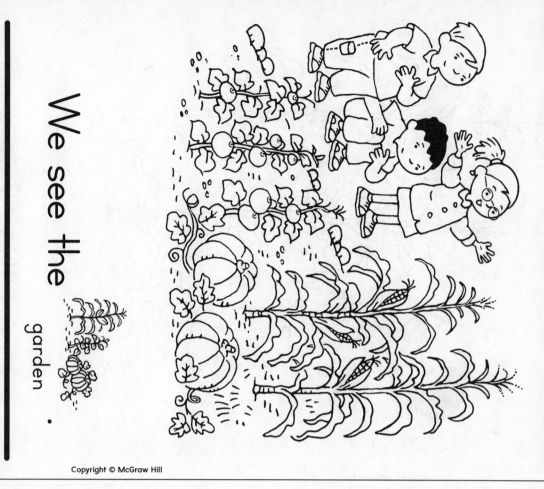

We see the
garden .

Connect to Community
Encourage children to read the story to a family member or a friend.

4

I See

I see the
worm .

High-Frequency Words: see
Have children set a purpose for reading, such as finding out what the children see. Then point out that reading moves from left to right. Have children demonstrate moving their finger from left to right as they read.

I

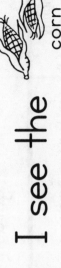

I see the .

corn

I see the  .

pumpkin

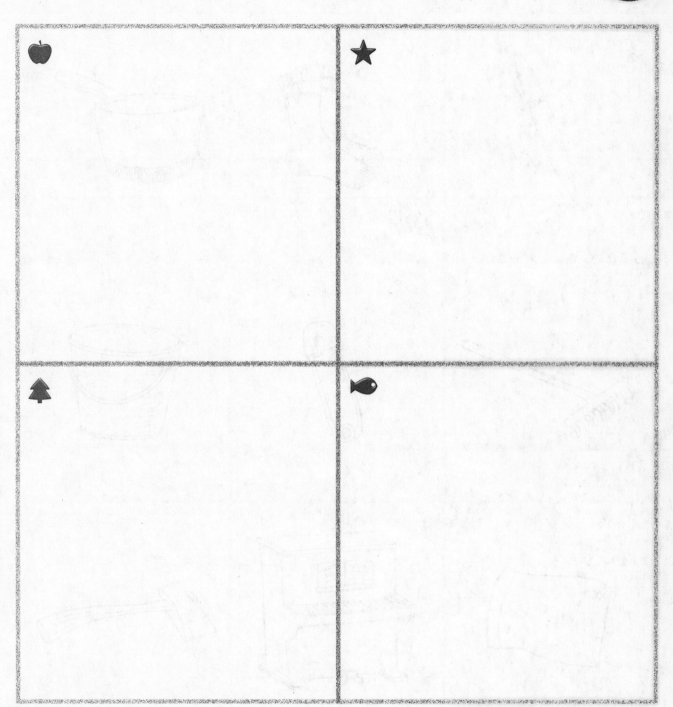

Phonological Awareness: Identify Alliteration

Explain to children that sometimes words in a sentence begin with the same sound. Say: *Sally sells socks.* Elicit from children that the words begin with the /s/ sound. Then say: *Sally runs fast* and point out that the words do not begin with the same sound. Model drawing a picture of a girl selling socks. Tell children you will say other sentences aloud. Tell them to draw a picture that describes the sentence that has the most words beginning with the same sound. 🍎 *Alice asked for apples. Alice ate bananas.* ⭐ *Put your games away. Put your pink pen away.* 🌲 *Larry has a leaping lizard. Larry has a soft bunny.* 🐟 *The big bunny bounced in the bin. The bunny ate a lot of carrots.*

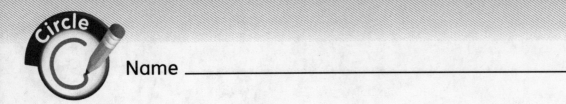
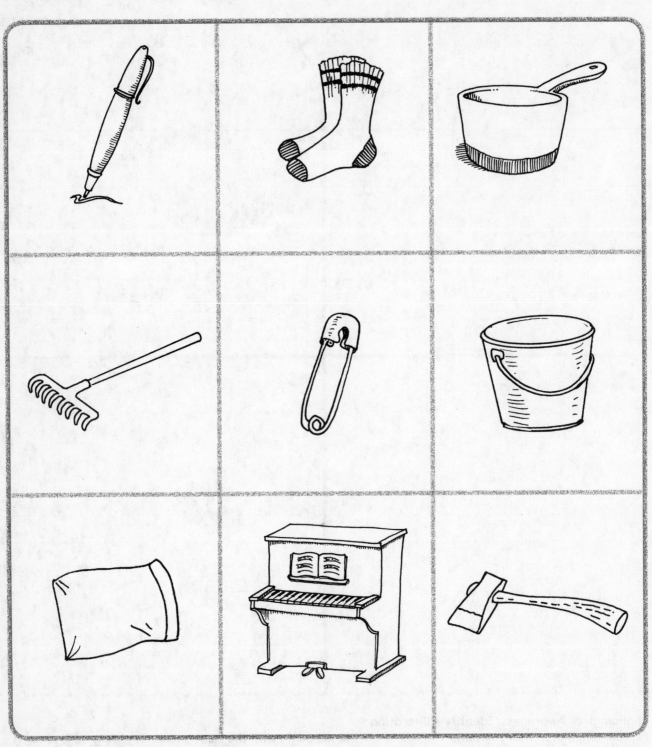

Phonemic Awareness: /p/

Point to and say the name of the picture of the pen in the first box and explain that *pen* begins with the /p/ sound. Have children repeat, *pen*, /p/. Then point to and say the names of the rest of the pictures on the page. Tell children to circle the pictures that have names that begin with the /p/ sound as in *pen*.

Name _____

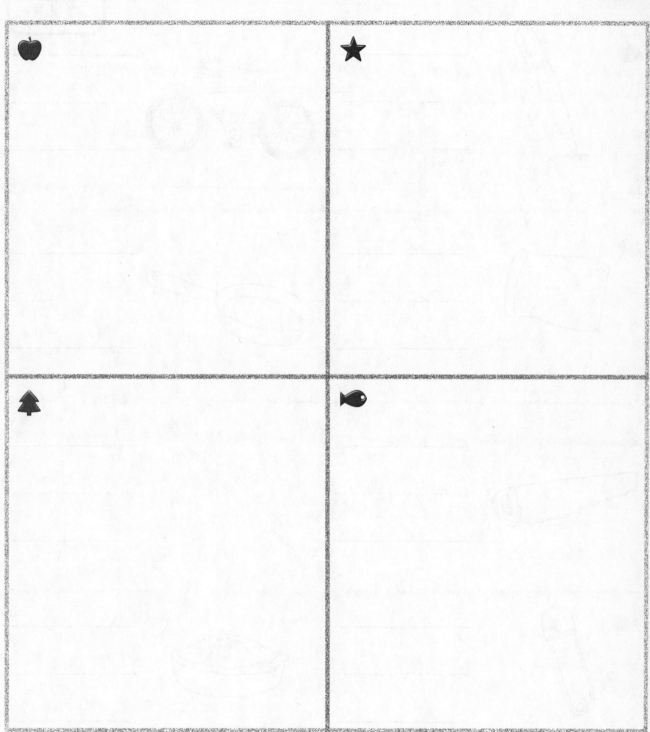

Phonemic Awareness: Phoneme Blending with /p/
Tell children to listen to the sounds in the word *pop*. Model blending the sounds to say the word *pop*, /poooop/, *pop*. Have children repeat. Then tell children you will say the sounds in more words. Have them blend the sounds to say each word. Then have them draw a picture of the word: I. /p//a//n/; 2. /p//i//g/; 3. /p//e//t/; 4. /p//o//t/ .

Name _____

Pp

🍎 _____

p

_____

⭐ _____

_____

🌲 _____

_____

🐟 _____

_____

Phonics: /p/p

Point to and say the word *pen* in the apple row. Say that it begins with the /p/ sound. Explain that the letter *p* stands for the /p/ sound. Now point to and say the names of the rest of the pictures. Have children write the letter *p* next to the picture if its name begins with the /p/ sound. Remind children to look at the pictures in each row from left to right and to work their way from the top to the bottom of the page.

sap   am   map

_____

_____

- - - - - - - - - - - - - - - - - -

_____

_____

- - - - - - - - - - - - - - - - - -

_____

Phonics/Spelling

Decode Words: Say *am* and point to your mouth position. Repeat with *Pam*. Write both words and model how to decode them. Then have children decode the words at the top of the page. Spell Words: Have children write the word that names each picture. Then dictate the words *am* and *sap* for children to spell. Model how to spell *am* by writing a letter for each sound. Then decode the word.

p

a

m

s

Phonics: Letter/Sound Match
Point to the *p* and explain to children that this letter stands for the /p/ sound. Model drawing a line from the letter *p* to the picture of the pan. Then say the name of each picture. Tell children to draw a line from each letter to the picture whose name begins with that letter.

Name _____

Pp

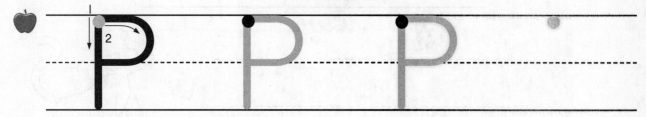

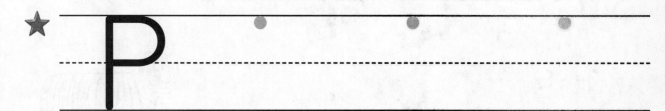

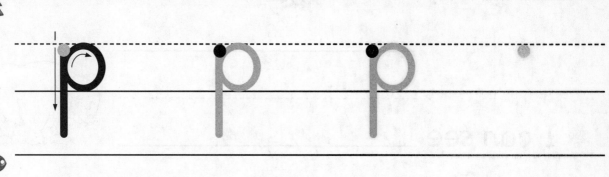

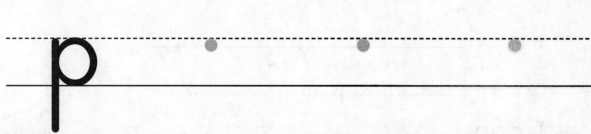

Handwriting: *Pp*
Demonstrate following the numbers and arrows to model for **children the** proper formation of the
uppercase and lowercase *Pp*. To form the uppercase letter *P* say: *Straight down. Go back to the top.*
Around and in at the dotted line. To form the lowercase letter *p* say: *Straight down, past the bottom line.*
Circle around all the way. Have children use their finger to trace the models for each of the letters. Then
have them write the uppercase and lowercase forms of the **letters** *Pp.*

Name _____

| a | see |

_____

🍎 We _____ a _____ .

_____

⭐ We see _____ .

_____

🌲 I can see _____ .

_____

🐟 I can _____ a _____ .

High-Frequency Words: *a, see*
Model the Read/Spell/Write routine with the word *a*. Have children repeat. Remind them that the other word in the box is *see*. Have children write a word from the box on the line to complete each sentence. Have partners read the sentences to each other. Then dictate the words *a* and *see* for children to spell.

Category Words: Colors

Explain that there are many colors. Say: *Red, green, yellow, and orange are colors.* Then say: *A tomato and a strawberry are red.* Then point to and name the pictures in each row. Have children circle the two pictures in each row that are the same color. Have partners tell what other things are the same color.

Name _____

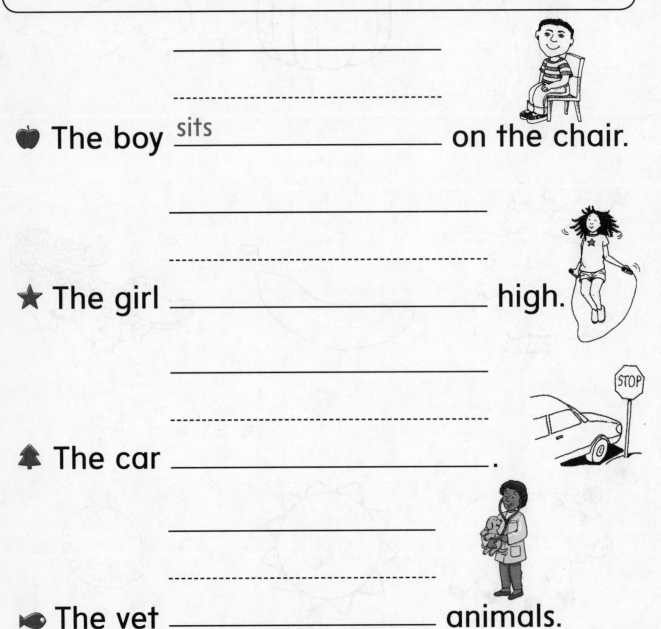

sits jumps stops helps

🍎 The boy _sits_____ on the chair.

⭐ The girl _____ high.

🌲 The car _____.

🐟 The vet _____ animals.

Grammar: Verbs
Explain to children that a verb is a word that shows an action. Point to and say the four verbs in the box.
Read the first sentence. Tell children you will choose a word from the box to complete the sentence. Then
write the word *sits* on the line. Then read each of the other sentences and talk about the pictures. Help
children choose a word from the box to complete each sentence.

Name _____

_____

- 🍎 The girl _____.

swims   book

- ⭐ Tim _____ fast.

fast   runs

- 🌲 The dog _____ its tail.

wags   cute

- 🐟 The baby _____.

loud   crawls

Grammar: Verbs
Remind children that a verb is a word that shows action. Say: *The word* jumps *is a verb because it tells about an action.* Encourage children to name different actions they make. Then point to and name the pictures on the page. Read each sentence and the two answer choices. Tell children to write the verb that completes each sentence. Tell children to refer back to a piece of writing that they did during the week and make sure they used verbs correctly.

Name _____

🍎 Isee a pie.

_____

- -

_____

⭐ We see a pig

_____

- -

_____

🌲 my brother tim is tall.

_____

- -

_____

🐟 we like the dog.

_____

- -

_____

Edit/Proofread
Tell children to listen as you read aloud the sentences. Remind children that a sentence, a person's name, and the letter I all begin with a capital letter and end with an end punctuation mark, such as a period. Have them rewrite each sentence so it shows correct capitalization and end punctuation. Remind children that they read and write from left to right.

86 Grade K • Unit 2 • Week I

I see a 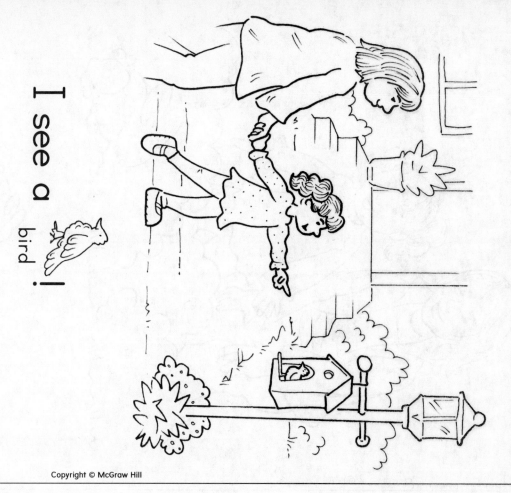 bird !

Connect to Community
Encourage children to read the story to a family member or a friend.

4

Grade K · Unit 2 · Week 1

▲ Walk

I see a 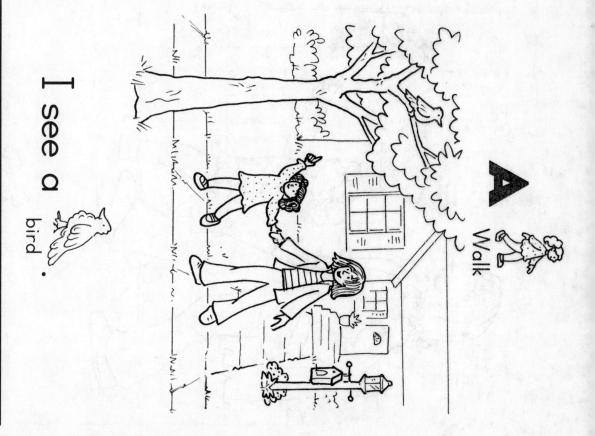 bird .

High-Frequency Words: *a*
Have children set a purpose for reading such as finding out what the little girl sees. Point to the space between each word on page 1. Then encourage children to point to the space between each word on page 3.

1

I see a 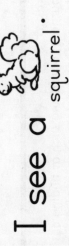 rabbit .

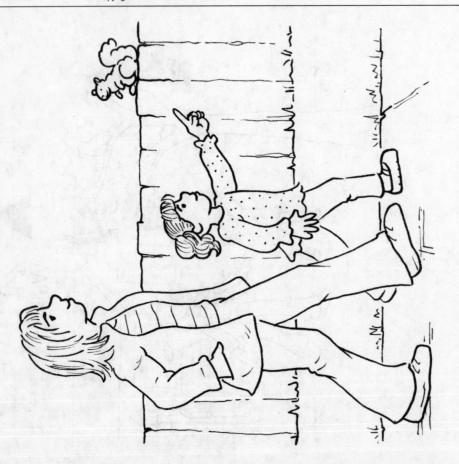

I see a squirrel.

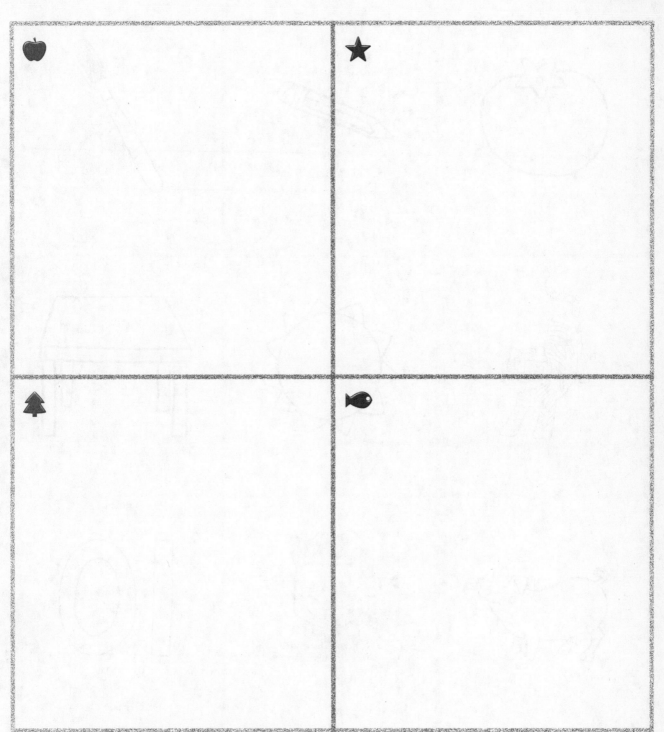

Phonological Awareness: Onset and Rime Blending
Say the word tap. Then say /t/ /ap/, *tap*. Have children repeat. Explain that you first said the very
beginning sound in the word *tap* and then you said the remaining sounds. Tell children that you will say the
beginning and ending sounds in some words. Tell them to blend the beginning and ending sounds together
to say the word. Then tell children to draw a picture of the word in each box. 🍎 /m//at/, *mat*; ⭐ /t//ub/,
tub; 🌲 /m//op, *mop*; 🐟 /h//at/, *hat*.

Phonemic Awareness: /t/
Point to and say the name of the picture of the tomato in the first box and explain that *tomato* begins with the /t/ sound. Have children repeat, *tomato*, /t/. Then point to and say the name of each picture on the page. Tell children to circle the pictures in each row that have names that begin with the /t/ sound.

Name _____

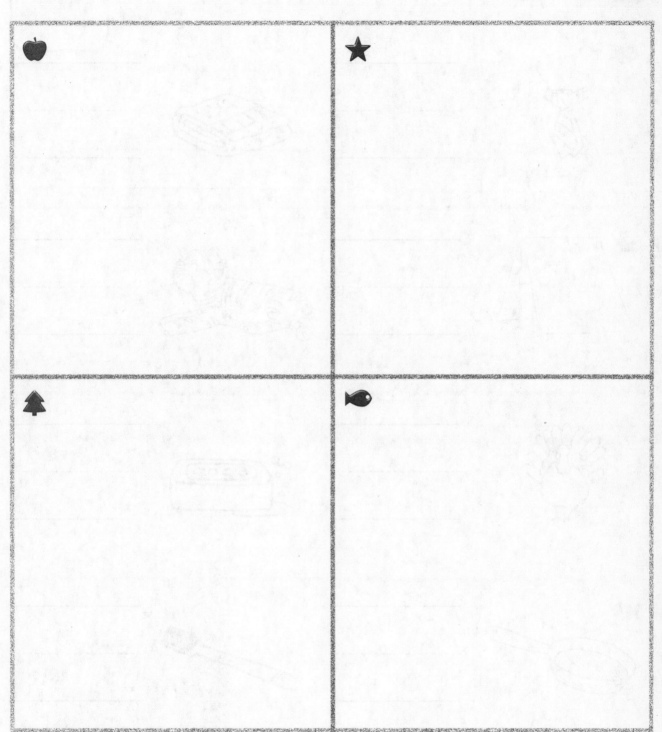

Phonemic Awareness: Phoneme Blending with /t/
Tell children to listen to the sounds in the word *tip*. Model blending the sounds to say the word *tip, /tiiip/,* *tip*. Have children repeat. Then tell children you will say the sounds in more words. Have them blend the sounds to say each word. Then have them draw a picture of the word: 🍎 /t//e//n/; ⭐ /c//a//t/; 🌲 /t//u//b/; 🐟 /t//o//p/.

Name _____

T t

Phonics: /t/ t

Point to and say the word *tie* in the apple row. Say that it begins with the /t/ sound. Explain that the letter *t* stands for the /t/ sound. Now point to and say the names of the rest of the pictures. Have children write the letter *t* next to the picture if its name begins with the /t/ sound as in *tie*. Remind children to look at the pictures in each row from left to right and to work their way from the top to the bottom of the page.

Name _____

Tam   am   tap   at

_____

- - - - - - - - - - - - - - - - - - -

- - - - - - - - - - - - - - - - - - -

Phonics/Spelling
Decode Words: Say *am* and point to your mouth position. **Repeat with** *Sam*. **Write both words and model**
how to decode them. Then have children decode the words at the top of the page. Spell Words: Then have
children write the word that names the first picture. Tell children that they should then write a word that
begins with /t/ that tells a girl's name. Say aloud the words *at, am,* and *sap* for children to spell.

Name _____

t

a

m

p

Copyright © McGraw Hill. Permission is granted to reproduce for classroom use.

Phonics: Letter/Sound Match
Point to the first letter and explain to children that this letter stands for the /t/ sound. Say the name of each picture. Then tell children to draw a line from each letter to the picture whose name begins with that letter.

94 Grade K • Unit 2 • Week 2

Name _____

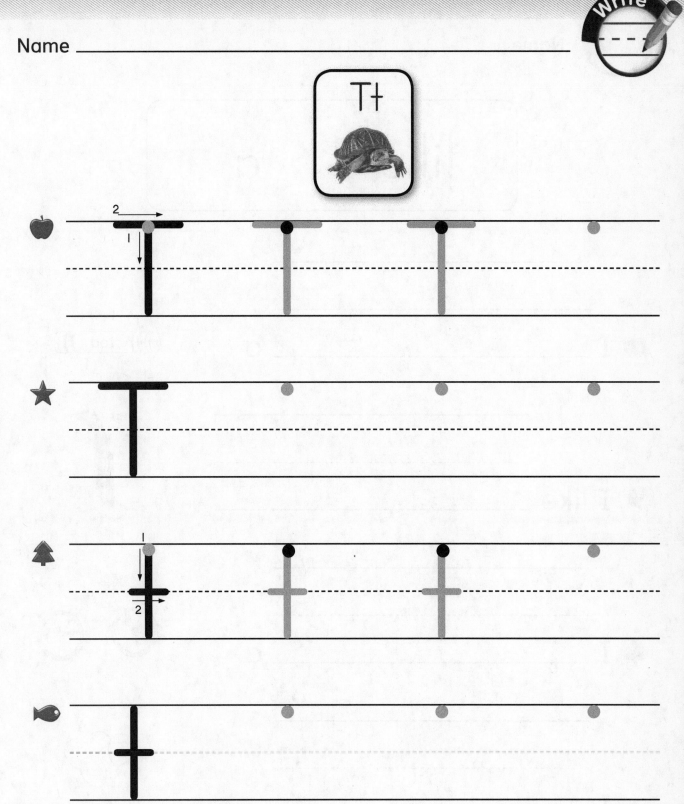

Handwriting: *Tt*

Demonstrate following the numbers and arrows to model for children the proper formation of the uppercase and lowercase *Tt*. To form the uppercase letter *T* say: *Straight down. Go back to the top. Straight across.* To form the lowercase letter *t* say: *Straight down. Go to the dotted line. Straight across.* Have children use their finger to trace the models for each of the letters. Then have them write the uppercase and lowercase forms of the letters *Tt*.

like   a

_____

- -

🍎 I _____ a   [red crayon] .

_____

- -

⭐ I like _____   [penguin] .

_____

- -

🌲 I _____ a   [bicycle] .

_____

- -

🐟 I _____   [balloons] .

High-Frequency Words: *like, a*
Model the Read/Spell/Write routine with *like*. Have children repeat. Remind children that the other word in the box is *a*. Have children then write a word from the box on the line to complete each sentence. Have partners read the sentences to each other. Dictate the words *like* and *a* for children to spell.

Name _____

  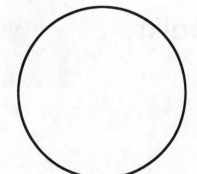 

 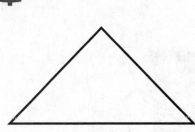  

Category Words: Shapes
Explain to children that things can be different shapes, such as a circle, square, triangle, or rectangle.
Tell children that some of the pictures on this page show different shapes. Point to and name the pictures
in each row. Have children circle the two pictures in each row that show shapes. Encourage children to use
shape words in sentences with a partner.

Name _____

🍎 The lion walks.

⭐ We dance.

🌲 I draw on the paper.

🐟 Pam plays with the dog.

Grammar: Verbs
Remind children that a verb is a word that names an action. Say: *The word* jump *is a verb*. Then read each sentence and point to and name the pictures. Tell children to circle the verb in each sentence. Then encourage children to refer back to a piece of writing that they did during the week and make sure they used verbs correctly.

_____

- -

🍎 **The boy** _____.

swims　　　water

_____

- -

⭐ **The tiger** _____.

growls　　　sleeps

_____

- -

🌲 **The man** _____.

jumps　　　hikes

_____

- -

🐟 **The girl** _____.

jumps　　　cute

Grammar: Verbs
Remind children that a verb tells about an action. Point to and name the pictures on the page. Then read each sentence and the two answer choices. Tell children to write the verb that completes each sentence.

Grade K • Unit 2 • Week 2 **99**

🍎 pam can see Sam.

_____

- - - - - - - - - - - - - - - - - - -

_____

⭐ Can I see pam?

_____

- - - - - - - - - - - - - - - - - - -

_____

🌲 Max can mix it

_____

- - - - - - - - - - - - - - - - - - -

_____

🐟 Tam can find it?

_____

- - - - - - - - - - - - - - - - - - -

_____

Edit/Proofread
Tell children to listen as you read aloud the sentences. Have them rewrite each sentence so it shows correct capitalization and end punctuation.

We like the shapes !

Connect to Community
Encourage children to read the story to a family member or a friend.

4

Grade K · Unit 2 · Week 2

We Like!

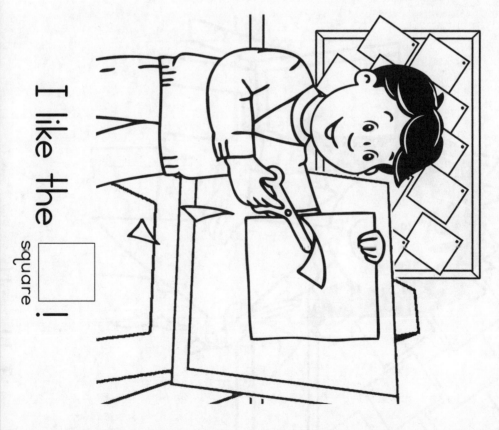

I like the ☐ square !

High-Frequency Words
Have children set a purpose for reading, such as to find out what the children like. Point to the space between each word on page 1. Then encourage children to point to the space between each word on page 3.

1

I like the ☐ rectangle.

I like the △ triangle.

3

2

Name _____

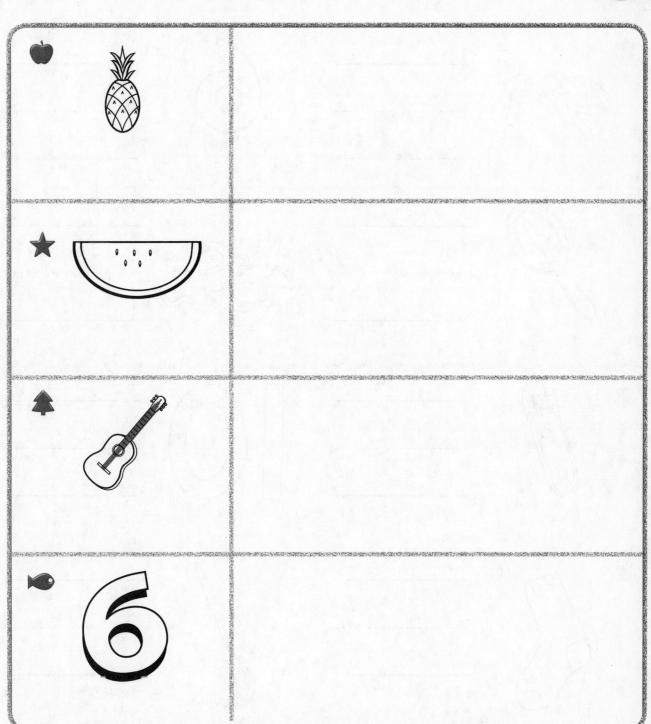

Phonological Awareness: Count and Segment Syllables
Point to the pineapple and say its name. Model clapping for each syllable or part in the word. Point out that there are three parts or syllables in *pineapple*. Tell children that you will write the number 3 in the box because *pineapple* has three parts or syllables. Point to and name the picture in each row. Tell children to write a number on the line to show how many parts or syllables they hear. Then have children identify the syllables or word parts in each word.

Review Phonics: /m/m, /a/a, /p/p, /s/s, /t/t
Point to and say the word *ant* in the apple row. Say that it begins with the /a/ sound. Explain that the letter *a* stands for the /a/ sound. Now point to and say the names of the rest of the pictures on the page. Have children write the letter that stands for the first sound in the picture name on the lines. Remind children to look at the pictures in each row from left to right and work their way from the top of the page to the bottom.

Name _____

_____

- - - - - - - - - - - - - -

_____

_____

- - - - - - - - - - - - - -

_____

_____

- - - - - - - - - - - - - -

_____

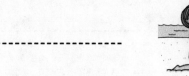

_____

- - - - - - - - - - - - - -

_____

_____

- - - - - - - - - - - - - -

_____

_____

- - - - - - - - - - - - - -

_____

Review Phonics: /m/m, /a/a, /p/p, /s/s, /t/t
Point to and say the name of each picture on the page. Then tell children to write the letter that stands for the first sound in the picture name on the line. Remind children to look at the pictures in each row from left to right and to work their way through the page from top to bottom.

Write

Name _____

Pam at tap Sam

Phonics/Spelling

Decode Words: Say *am* and point to your mouth position. Repeat with *sat*. Write both words and model how to decode them by saying the sounds in each word and then blending them together to say each word. Then have children decode the words at the top of the page. Spell Words: Tell children to write the word that names the picture on the lines. Then dictate the words *mat, sat, at, am,* and *Tam* for children to spell.

106 Grade K • Unit 2 • Week 3

Name _____

🍎   **a**   **like**   **see**

⭐   **we**   **the**   **a**

🌲   **the**   **like**   **we**

🐟   **see**   **a**   **the**

Review High-Frequency Words
Have children follow these directions:
🍎 Circle the word *see*.   ⭐ Circle the word *the*.
🌲 Circle the word *we*.   🐟 Circle the word *a*.
Dictate the words *the, we, see, a,* and *like* for children to spell.

Name _____

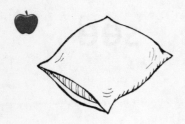  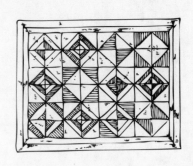

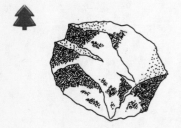  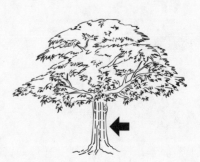

Category Words: Textures

Explain to children that things can feel differently. Say: *Cotton* is soft but a *book* is hard. *Silk* is a smooth fabric. *Sandpaper* is rough.

🍎 Circle the pictures of things that are soft.
⭐ Circle the pictures of things that are hard.
🌲 Circle the pictures of things that are rough.

Encourage children to use texture words in sentences with a partner.

108 Grade K • Unit 2 • Week 3

Name _____

Category Words Review
 Circle the pictures in this row that show feelings.
★ Circle the pictures in this row that show shapes.
🌲 Circle the pictures in this row that show things that are yellow.
Encourage children to use feeling, shape, and color words in sentences with a partner.

Grade K • Unit 2 • Week 3 **109**

Name _____

🍎 We dance to the music.

★ The frog jumps.

🌲 He runs fast.

🐟 The boy rides the bike.

Grammar: Verbs
Remind children that a verb is a word that tells about an action. Say: *The word* eats *is a verb because it tells about an action, or what someone is doing.* The words *walks* and *hops* are verbs. Tell children to listen to each sentence and circle the verb in each one. Then have children refer back to a piece of writing that they did during the week and make sure they used verbs or action words correctly.

🍎 **The child** _____ .

short   writes

⭐ **Pam** _____ .

jumps   up

🌲 **The frog** _____ .

far   leaps

🐟 **The man** _____ .

fishes   rod

Grammar: Verbs
Point to and name the pictures on the page. Then read each sentence and the two answer choices. Tell children to write the verb that completes each sentence on the line.

Name _____

🍎 Can i sit?

_____

_____

⭐ we like to nap.

_____

🌲 Nat Can pat the cat.

_____

🐟 We can go?

_____

Edit/Proofread
Tell children to listen as you read aloud the sentences. Have them rewrite each sentence so each one shows correct capitalization and end punctuation.

See the Bugs !

We see a bee **.**

We like the bugs **!**

Connect to Community
Encourage children to read the story to a family member or a friend.

Review High-Frequency Words: *the, a, see, we, like*
Have children set a purpose for reading, such as finding out what the children see. Point to the space between each word on page 1. Then encourage children to point to the space between each word on page 2.

We see a butterfly.

We see a caterpillar.

Phonological Awareness: Identify Rhyme
Remind children that words that rhyme have the same ending sounds. Now point to and say the names of the pictures in each row on the page. Have children circle the two pictures in each row that have names that rhyme.

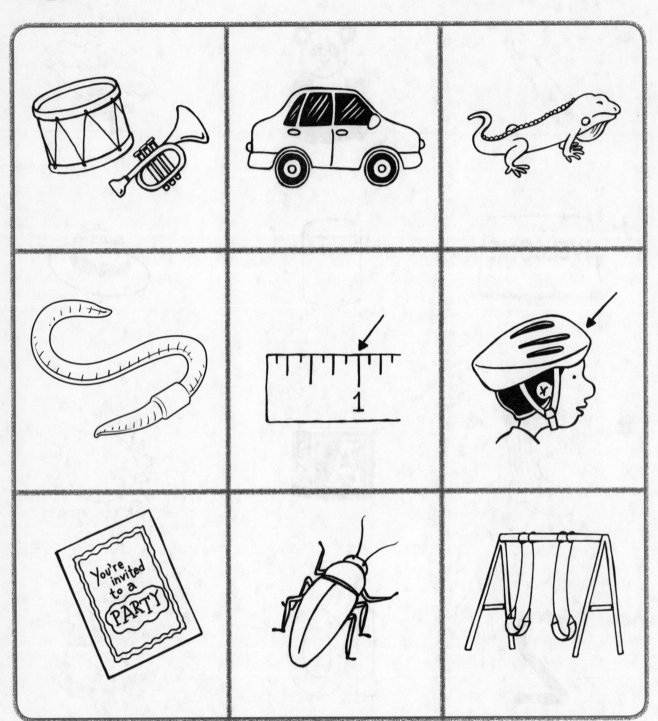

Phonemic Awareness: /i/
Point to and say the name of the picture of the instruments. Tell children that the word *instruments* begins with the /i/ sound. Have children repeat, *instruments*, /i/. Now point to and say the names of the rest of the pictures on the page. Tell children to circle the pictures that have names that begin with the /i/ sound as in *instruments*. Tell children to look at the pictures in each row from left to right and work their way down the page from top to bottom.

Name _____

Draw

Phonemic Awareness: Phoneme Blending with /i/
Tell children to listen to the sounds in the word *tip*. Model blending the sounds to say the word *tip*, /tiiip/, *tip*. Have children repeat. Then tell children you will say the sounds in more words. Have them blend the sounds to say each word. Then have them draw a picture of the word: ● /p//i//n/; ★ /m//i//t/; ♠ /t//u//b/; ➤ /t//o//p/.

Name _____

 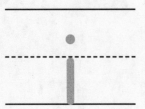 _____  _____

 _____  _____

  _____  _____

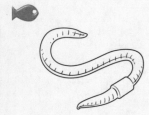 _____   _____

Phonics: /i/ i

Point to and say the word *inch* in the apple row. Say that it begins with the /i/ sound. Explain that the letter *i* stands for the /i/ sound. Now point to and say the names of the rest of the pictures on the page. Have children write the letter *i* next to the picture if its name begins with the /i/ sound as in *inch*. Remind children to look at the pictures in each row from left to right and work their way from the top of the page to the bottom.

118 Grade K • Unit 3 • Week 1

it   sat   tip   sip

_____

_____
- -
_____

_____
- -
_____

Phonics/Spelling
Decode Words: Say *it* and point to your mouth position. Write *it* and model how to decode it. Then have children decode the words at the top of the page. Spell Words: Have children write the word that names each picture on the lines. Then say the words *it* and *at* for children to spell.

Name _____

i

m

a

t

p

Phonics: Letter/Sound Match

Point to the first letter and explain to children that this letter stands for the /i/ sound. Say the name of each picture. Point out that *insect* starts with the /i/ sound so you will draw a line from the letter *i* to the insect. Then tell children to draw a line from each letter to the picture whose name begins with that letter and sound. Have children identify the sound for each letter.

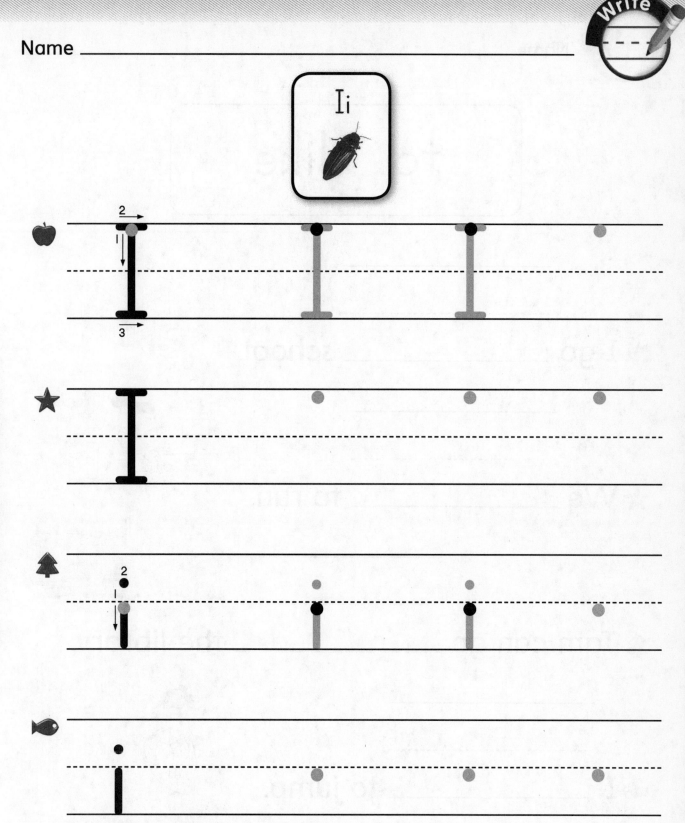

Handwriting: *Ii*

Demonstrate to children the proper formation of the uppercase and lowercase *Ii*. For the uppercase *I,* say: *Straight down. Go back to the top. Straight across. Go to the bottom line. Straight across.* For the lowercase *i* say: *Straight down, dot above.* Have children use their finger to trace the model for the letter. Then have them write the uppercase and lowercase forms of the letter *Ii*.

Name _____

to like

_____

- - - - - - - - - - - - - - - - - - -

🍎 I go _____ school.

_____

- - - - - - - - - - - - - - - - -

⭐ We _____ to run.

_____

- - - - - - - - - - - - - - - - - - -

🌲 Tam can go _____ the library.

_____

- - - - - - - - - - - - - - - -

🐟 I _____ to jump.

High-Frequency Words: *to, like*
Model the Read/Spell/Write routine using the word *to*. Have children repeat the routine. Point to the word *like* and have children read it. Point to and name the pictures on the page. Then tell children to write the word that completes each sentence on the lines. Have partners read the phrases to each other. Say aloud the words *to* and *like* for children to spell.

Name _____

Category Words: Action Words
Explain to children that people and animals can move. Say that the words *walk* and *hop* are action words. Tell children that some of the pictures on this page show someone or something moving. Point to and name the pictures in each row. Have children circle the two pictures in each row that show someone or something moving. Encourage pairs of children to use the action words in sentences.

Name _____

🍎 **The puppy runs to the flowers.**

⭐ **has pretty pink flowers**

🌲 **Zack wrote a story.**

🐟 **the cute little baby**

Grammar: Sentences
Explain to children that a sentence tells a complete idea. Say: *The children play* is a complete sentence. Explain that a sentence always begins with a capital letter and has an end mark, such as a period. Then say: *play in the park* is not a sentence because it does not tell a complete idea. Then read each example and point to and name the pictures. Tell children to circle the example if it is a complete sentence. Tell children to refer back to a piece of writing they did during the week and make sure it tells a complete idea and has correct capitalization and end punctuation.

Name _____

🍎 I wear a seatbelt in the car.

★ We follow the rules of the game.

🌲 big dog barks.

🐟 The nice teacher.

Grammar: Sentences
Read each example and point to and name the pictures. Tell children to circle the example if it is a complete sentence. Use gestures to clarify meaning.

🍎 **Can tim tap?**

_____

- -

_____

⭐ **Sam can sit**

_____

- -

_____

🌲 **Did Pam tap.**

_____

- -

_____

🐟 **can we run.**

_____

- -

_____

Edit/Proofread

Tell children to listen as you read aloud the sentences. Have them rewrite each sentence so it shows correct capitalization and punctuation. Use gestures to clarify meaning. Tell children to refer back to a piece of writing that they did during the week and make sure they used correct capitalization and end punctuation. Tell children to also check to see that they used spelling patterns to help them spell words correctly.

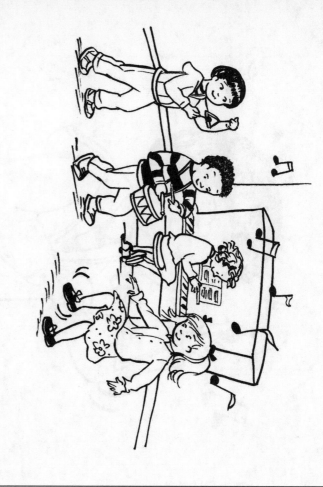

I like to tap to the 🎵 !

music

Connect to Community
Encourage children to read the story to a family member or a friend.

We Like to Tap

I like to tap the 🎹 .

piano

Review High-Frequency Words
Have children set a purpose for reading, such as finding out what instruments the children like to tap. Explcin that words in a sentence are separated by spaces. Point to the space between the words *to* and *tap* on page I. Then ask children to point to the space between the words *like* and *to* on page 4.

I like to tap the .

I like to tap the 🥁.
drum

Name _____

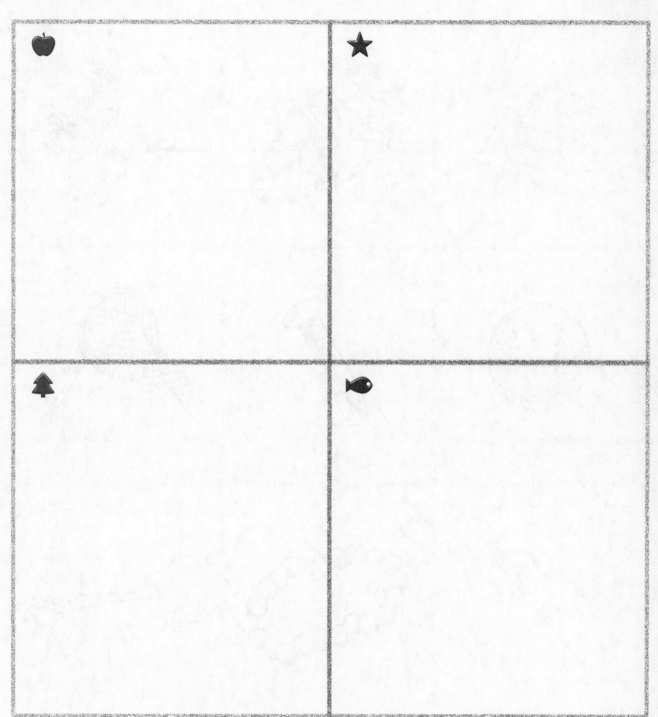

Phonological Awareness: Onset and Rime Blending

Say the word *nap*. Then say /n//ap/, *nap*. Have children repeat. Explain that you first said the beginning sound in the word *nap* and then you said the remaining sounds. Say that you blended the sounds together to say *nap*. Tell children that you will say the beginning and ending sounds in some words. Have them blend the sounds together to say the word. Then tell children to draw a picture of the word in each box. 🍎 /n//et/, *net*; ⭐ /t//en/, *ten*; 🌲 /p//an/, *pan*; 🐟 /p//in/, *pin*.

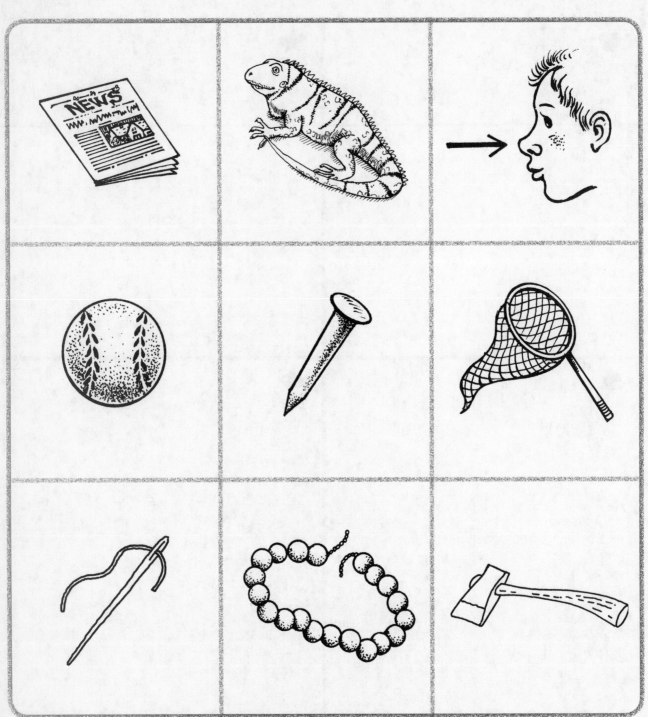

Phonemic Awareness: /n/

Point to and say the name of the picture of the newspaper. Tell children that the word *newspaper* begins with the /n/ sound. Have children repeat, *newspaper*, /n/. Now point to and say the names of the rest of the pictures on the page. Tell children to circle the pictures that have names that begin with the /n/ sound as in *newspaper*.

Name _____

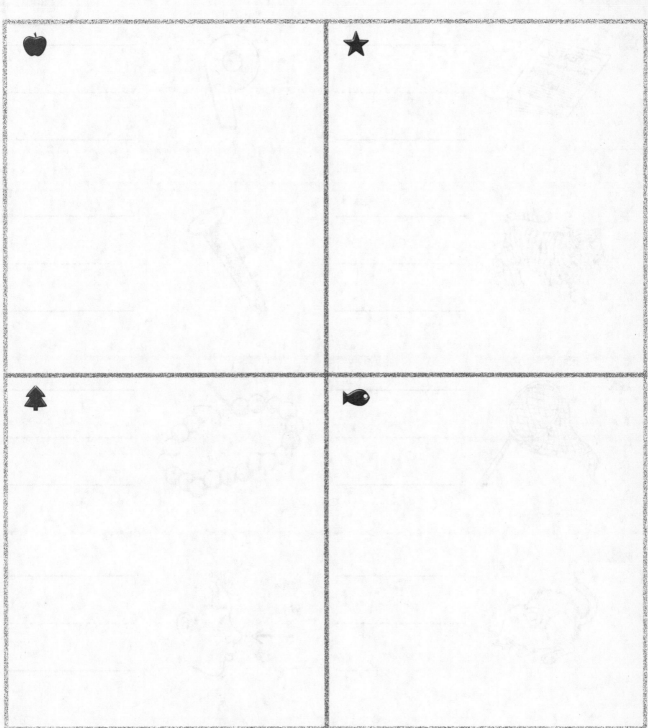

Phonemic Awareness: Phoneme Blending with /n/
Tell children to listen to the sounds in the word *Nat*. Model blending the sounds to say the word *Nat*
/nnnaaat/, *Nat*. Have children repeat. Then tell children you will say the sounds in more words. Have
them blend the sounds to say each word. Then have them draw a picture of the word: 🍎 /n//e//t/;
⭐ /p//e//n/; 🌲 /n//u//t/; 🐟 /p//a//n/.

n 9

Phonics: /n/n
Point to and say the name of the picture of the newspaper. Tell children that the word *newspaper* begins with the /n/ sound. Explain that the letter *n* stands for the /n/ sound. Now point to and say the name of the rest of the pictures on the page. Have children write the letter *n* next to the picture if its name begins with the /n/ sound as in *newspaper*. Tell children to look at the pictures in each row from left to right. Then tell them to work their way from the top of the page to the bottom.

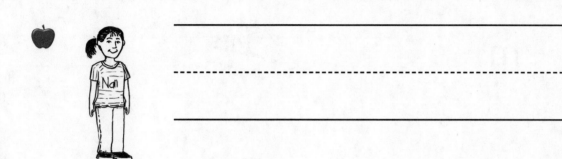

in   tan   it   pin

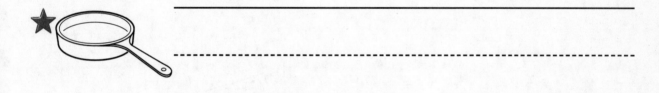

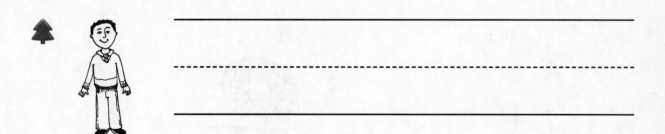

Phonics/Spelling

Decode Words: Say *tin*. Point out that there are three sounds: /t/ /i/ /n/. Explain that the letters *t, i, n* stand for the sounds. Repeat with *nap*. Write both words and model how to decode them. Then have children decode the words at the top of the page. Spell Words: Model how to spell the words *at* and *mat* by writing a letter for each sound. Then decode the words. Say: *Some words end with the same sounds and spelling pattern, such as* at *and* mat. *Use a spelling pattern to write the picture names.*

Name _____

n

m

i

t

p

Phonics: Letter/Sound Match
Point to the first letter and explain to children that this letter stands for the /n/ sound. Say the name of each picture. Then tell children to draw a line from each letter to the picture whose name begins with that letter.

Name _____

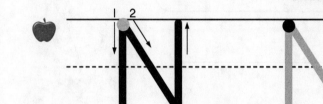

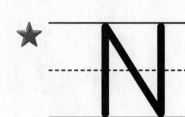

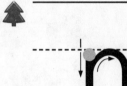

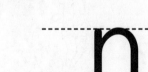

Handwriting

Demonstrate to children the proper formation of the uppercase and lowercase *Nn*. For the uppercase *N* say: *Straight down. Go back to the top. Slant down. Straight up.* For the lowercase *n* say: *Straight down. Around and straight down.* Have children use their finger to trace the model for the letter. Then have them write the uppercase and lowercase forms of the letter *Nn*.

Write

Name _____

and   to

_____

🍎 The boy can run _____ kick.

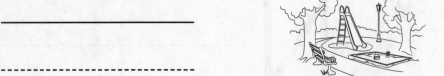

_____

⭐ We can go _____ the playground.

_____

🌲 I can read _____ write.

_____

🐟 Do you like _____ jump?

High-Frequency Words: *and, to*
Model the Read/Spell/Write routine using the word *and*. Have children repeat the routine. Remind children that the other word in the box is *to*. Tell children to repeat. Have children then write a word from the box on a line to complete each sentence. Have partners read the sentences to each other. Then say the words *and* and *to* aloud for children to spell. Tell children to make sure they spelled the words correctly.

Name _____

Category Words: Sound Words
Explain to children that people, animals, and things make sounds. Point to and name the pictures in each row. Have children circle the two pictures in each row that show someone or something making a sound.

🍎 **hear the sounds from the sky.**

★ **The school band played.**

🌲 **In the barn.**

🐟 **The bird can talk.**

Grammar: Sentences

Remind children that a sentence tells a complete idea. Say: *A sentence begins with a capital letter and ends with a punctuation mark, such as a period.* Read each example and point to and name the pictures. Tell children to circle the example if it is a complete sentence. Use gestures to clarify meaning.

🍎 **The dog barks.**

⭐ lives in the ocean

🌲 **My mom is a doctor.**

🐟 can beep

Grammar: Sentences

Remind children that a sentence tells a complete idea. It usually contains a noun and a verb. Say: *For example, some sentences tell a fact about someone or something and have a period at the end.* Read each example. Tell children to circle each example that is a complete sentence. Remind children also that a sentence begins with an uppercase letter and has end punctuation. Then have children refer back to a piece of writing they did during the week and make sure they used complete sentences and correct capitalization and that they added a period at the end of sentences that tell facts.

🍎 **Nat and Pam s i t.**

⭐ **Nan cansee a man.**

🌲 **We like the can and the pan**

🐟 **can you nap on the mat.**

Edit/Proofread
Tell children to listen as you read aloud the sentences. Have them rewrite each sentence so it shows correct capitalization and punctuation. Use gestures to clarify meaning. Tell children to refer back to a piece of writing that they did during the week and make sure they used correct capitalization and end punctuation.

Name _____

Grade K · Unit 3 · Week 2

Connect to Community
Encourage children to read the story to a family member or a friend.

Sam and Pam see it.

The Map

Sam and Pam draw .

Review High-Frequency Words
Have children set a purpose for reading, such as finding out what the children do with the map. Explain that words are made up of letters. Model by pointing to the word *and* on page 1 and then to the letter *a* in the word. Then ask children to point to a word on page 4 and then to a letter in the word.

1

Sam and Pam run .

Sam and Pam  read it.

Name _____

Phonological Awareness: Count and Segment Syllables

Point to the table and say its name. Model clapping for each syllable in the word. Point out that there are two parts or syllables in *table*. Tell children that you will write the number 2 in the box because *table* has two parts or syllables. Point to and name the remaining pictures. Tell children to say the parts in each word and write a number on the line to show how many parts or syllables they hear.

Phonemic Awareness: /k/c

Point to and say the name of the picture of the cat. Tell children that the word *cat* begins with the /k/ sound. Have children repeat, *cat*, /k/. Now point to and say the names of the rest of the pictures on the page. Tell children to circle the pictures that have names that begin with the /k/ sound as in *comb*. Tell children to look at the pictures in each row from left to right and work their way down the page from top to bottom.

144 Grade K • Unit 3 • Week 3

Name _____

Phonemic Awareness: /k/c

Point to and say the name of the pictures on the page. Tell children to circle the pictures that have names that begin with the /k/ sound as in *cut*. Tell children to look at the pictures in each row from left to right and work their way down the page from top to bottom.

Name _____

Cc

C

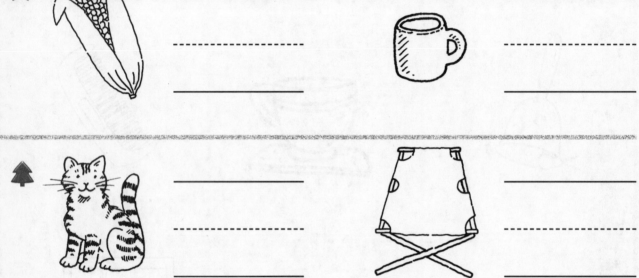

Phonics: /k/c

Point to and say the name of the picture of the comb. Tell children that the word *comb* begins with the /k/ sound. Explain that the letter *c* stands for the /k/ sound. Now point to and say the name of the rest of the pictures on the page. Have children write the letter *c* next to the picture if its name begins with /k/ sound as in *comb*. Tell children to look at the pictures in each row from left to right. Then tell them to work their way from the top of the page to the bottom.

146 Grade K • Unit 3 • Week 3

can tap Cam pin

_____

Phonics/Spelling

Decode Words: Say *Cam* and point to your mouth position. Write the word and model how to decode it as you say each sound in the name and then blend the sounds together to say *Cam*. Then have children decode the words at the top of the page. Spell Words: Have children write the word that names each picture.

c

s

p

t

i

Phonics
Point to the first letter and explain to children that this letter stands for the /k/ sound. Say the name of each picture. Then tell children to draw a line from each letter to the picture whose name begins with that letter.

148 Grade K • Unit 3 • Week 3

Name _____

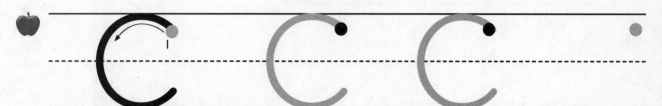

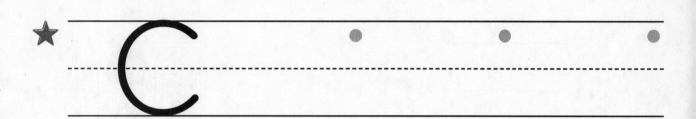

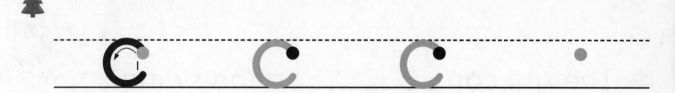

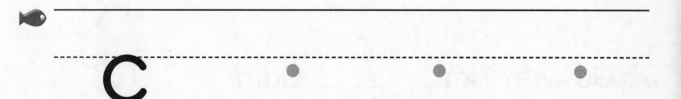

Handwriting: *Cc*
Demonstrate to children the proper formation of the uppercase and lowercase *Cc*. For the uppercase
C say: *Circle back and around, then stop.* For the lowercase *c* say: *Circle back and around, then stop.*
Have children use their finger to trace the model for the letter. Then have them write the uppercase and
lowercase forms of the letter *Cc*.

go   and

_____
- - - - - - - - - - - - - - - - -

🍎 I can _____ to school.

_____
- - - - - - - - - - - - - - - - -

⭐ You _____ I like to read.

_____
- - - - - - - - - - - - - - - - -

🌲 The girl can _____ on the swing.

_____
- - - - - - - - - - - - - - - - -

🐟 Go with Tim _____ Cam.

High-Frequency Words: *go, and*
Model the Read/Spell/Write routine using the word *go*. Have children repeat the routine. Remind children that the other word in the box is *and*. Tell children to repeat. Have children then write a word from the box on a line to complete each sentence. Have partners read the sentences to each other. Then say the words *go* and *and* aloud for children to spell. Tell children to make sure they spelled the words correctly.

_____

- - - - - - - - - - - - - - - - - -

_____

_____

- - - - - - - - - - - - - - - - - -

_____

_____

- - - - - - - - - - - - - - - - - -

_____

Category Words: Sequence Words

Explain that things happen in a certain order. Tell children that on a school day, for example, they first wake up, then get dressed, and finally they eat breakfast before going to school. Explain that the pictures on this page show the steps in making apple cake to sell at a market. Point to and describe each picture. Have children look at the pictures and write a number for what happens first, next, and last. Encourage partners to use these words as they talk about the order of the pictures.

Name _____

🍎 **Where is the library?**

⭐ **reads many books there.**

🌲 **What is your favorite book?**

🐟 **plays soccer?**

Grammar: Sentences
Remind children that a sentence tells a complete idea. A sentence begins with a capital letter and ends with a punctuation mark, such as a period, a question mark, or an exclamation mark. Then read each example and point to and name the pictures. Tell children to circle the example if it is a complete sentence. Then tell children to refer to a piece of writing that they did during the week and make sure they used correct capitalization and end punctuation. Tell children to also use spelling patterns to help them write words as well as use the correct spelling of high-frequency words.

Name _____

_____

- -

🍎 _____ lives at the zoo?

Who   **When**

_____

- -

⭐ _____ is the zoo?

When   **Where**

_____

- -

🌲 _____ does the play start?

Who   **When**

Grammar: Sentences
Explain that some sentences ask questions. Some question words are *Who, When, Where, How*. Then read
the sentences and word choices. Point to and say the name of each picture. Then tell children to write
the word that completes each sentence on the lines. Use gestures to clarify meaning. Tell children to refer
back to a piece of writing that they did during the week and make sure they used question marks in their
sentences correctly.

🍎 Can Nan see the cat.

_____

- -

_____

⭐ The cat can nap on the Mat.

_____

- -

_____

🌲 Can Tim see the cap.

_____

- -

_____

🐟 Go with me?

_____

- -

_____

Edit/Proofread
Tell children to listen as you read aloud the sentences. Have them rewrite each sentence so it shows correct capitalization and punctuation. Remind children that a sentence begins with an uppercase letter and ends with an end punctuation mark, such as a period or question mark. Say that a sentence tells a complete idea. Use gestures to clarify meaning.

We go
home .

Connect to Community
Encourage children to read the story to a family member or a friend.

We Go

We go to the
store .

Review High-Frequency Words
Have children set a purpose for reading, such as finding out where the bears go. Then tell children that they read from left to right. Model this concept of directionality for children.

We go to the 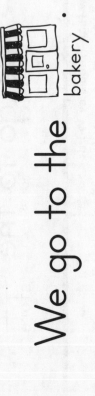 park

We go to the bakery

Name _____

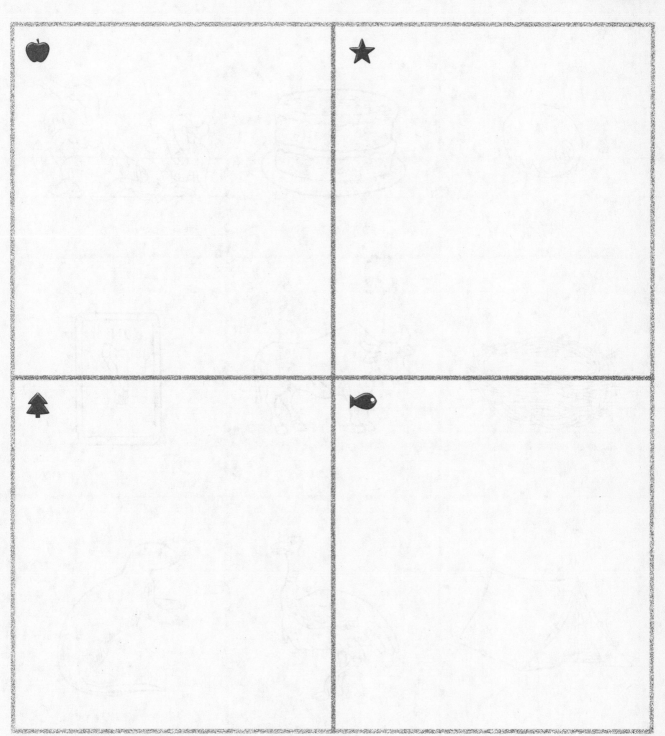

Phonological Awareness: Onset and Rime Segmentation

Explain to children that words are made up of beginning and ending sounds. Say the word *sit*. Tell children that the beginning sound is /s/. Then say that the ending sounds are /iiit/, *it*. Tell children to say the word, *sit*. Tell children that you will draw a picture of a person sitting in the first box. Then say some words and encourage children to say the beginning and ending sounds in each word. Have children draw a picture in each box that shows the word. ★ *sad, /s//ad/;* 🌲 *mat, /m//at/;* 🐟 *sun, /s//un/.*

Name _____

Phonemic Awareness: /o/ o

Point to and say the name of the picture of the olive. Tell children that the word *olive* begins with the /o/ sound. Have children repeat, *olive*, /o/. Now point to and say the names of the rest of the pictures on the page. Tell children to circle the pictures that have names that begin with the /o/ sound as in *olive*. Tell children to look at the pictures in each row from left to right and work their way down the page from top to bottom.

Name _____

1.	2.
3.	4.

Phonemic Awareness: Phoneme Blending with /o/
Tell children to listen to the sounds in the word *on*. Model blending the sounds to say the word *on*, /ooonnn/, *on*. Have children repeat. Then tell children you will say the sounds in more words. Have them blend the sounds to say each word. Then have them draw a picture of the word: 1. /p//o//t/; 2. /d//o//t/;
3. /p//i//n/; 4. /m//o//p/.

Name _____

1.

2.

3.

4.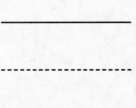

Phonics: /o/o

Point to and say the word *ostrich* in the apple row. Say that it begins with the /o/ sound. Explain that the letter *o* stands for the /o/ sound. Now point to and say the names of the rest of the pictures on the page. Have children write the letter *o* next to the picture if its name begins with the /o/ sound as in *ostrich*. Remind children to look at the pictures in each row from left to right and work their way from the top of the page to the bottom.

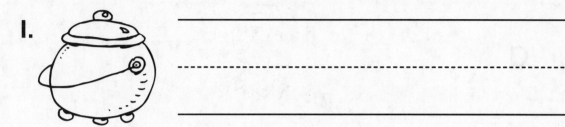

on   pop   can   cot

1. 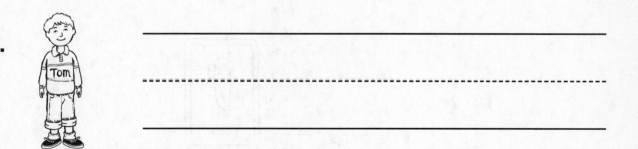 _____

- -

_____

2. _____

- -

_____

3. _____

- -

_____

Phonics/Spelling

Decode Words: Say *not* and point to your mouth position. Write *not* and model how to decode it by saying each sound and then blending the sounds together to say *not*. Repeat with *in* and *on*. Then have children decode the words at the top of the page. Spell Words: Have children write the word that names each picture.

o

a

c

n

i

Phonics
Point to the first letter and explain to children that this letter stands for the /o/ sound. Say the name of each picture. Then tell children to draw a line from each letter to the picture whose name begins with that letter.

1.

2.

3.

4.

Handwriting: *Oo*

Demonstrate to children the proper formation of the uppercase and lowercase *Oo*. For the uppercase *O* say: *Circle back, then around all the way*. For the lowercase *o*, repeat: *Circle back, then around all the way*. Have children use their finger to trace the model for the letter. Then have them write the uppercase and lowercase forms of the letter *Oo*.

 Write

Name _____

you   go

_____

1. _____ can plant the seeds.

2. You _____ to the party.

3. _____ can swim.

4. _____ can cook.

High-Frequency Words: _you, go_
Model the Read/Spell/Write routine using the word _you_. Have children repeat the routine. Remind children that the other word in the box is _go_. Tell children to repeat. Have children then write a word from the box on a line to complete each sentence. Have partners read the sentences to each other. Then say the words _you_ and _go_ for children to spell.

Name _____

1.

2.

3.

Category Words: Jobs Words
Explain to children that people can do different kinds of jobs. Tell them that you are a teacher which is a kind of job. Point to and name the pictures in each row. Have children look at the pictures in each row and circle the two pictures that show people doing jobs.

Name _____

1. We go to a big school.

2. I see a tiny mouse.

3. He ate a juicy orange.

4. The little baby crawls to me.

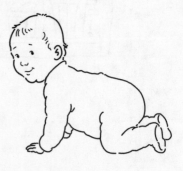

Grammar: Adjectives
Explain to children that an adjective describes something. Tell them that the word *funny* describes the book when you say *The funny book makes me laugh.* Then read each example and point to and name the pictures. Tell children to circle the adjective in each sentence.

Name _____

| big hot tall blue |

_____

1. I see the _____ clouds.

_____

2. I sit under a _____ tree.

_____

3. The _____ sun shines on me.

_____

4. Did you see the _____ crayon?

Grammar: Adjectives
Remind children that an adjective describes something or someone. Say: *Listen to this sentence*: The funny book made me laugh! *The word* funny *is an adjective*. It describes the book. Read the sentences and point to and name the pictures. Tell children to write a word from the box to complete each sentence. Tell children to refer back to a piece of writing that they did during the week and make sure they used adjectives correctly.

1. I can see Mom

---

2. Can Sam go to the top.

---

3. You can tap

---

4. Tim and Nat can play?

Edit/Proofread
Tell children to listen as you read aloud the sentences. Have them rewrite each sentence so it shows correct capitalization and punctuation. Use gestures to clarify meaning. Then have children refer to a piece of writing that they did during the week and make sure they used correct capitalization and end punctuation.

Name _____

You and I can pull !

Connect to Community
Encourage children to read the story to a family member or a friend.

Grade K • Unit 4 • Week 1

4

Copyright © McGraw Hill

You and I

You and I can rake .

Review High-Frequency Words
Have children set a purpose for reading, such as finding out what the children do in the garden. Point to the letter *u* in the word *you* on page 1. Tell children that words are made up of letters. Say that the letter *u* is a letter in the word *you*. Then ask children to point to letter *u* in the word *can* on page 4.

1

You and I can  water .

You and I can  dig .

1.			
2.			
3.			
4.			

Phonological Awareness: Sentence Segmentation

Remind children that sentences are made up of words. Say: *I like my neighborhood.* Tell children that there are four words in the sentence. Hold up a finger for each word in the sentence. Tell children you will color in four boxes to show that there are four words in the sentence. Then tell children to color in a box for each word that they hear in the following sentences: 2. *I have friendly neighbors.* 3. *The store opened.* 4. *Buy it!* .

Phonemic Awareness: /d/

Point to and say the name of the picture of the desk. Tell children that the word *desk* begins with the /d/ sound. Have children repeat, *desk*, /d/. Now point to and say the names of the rest of the pictures on the page. Tell children to circle the pictures that have names that begin with the /d/ sound as in *desk*. Tell children to look at the pictures in each row from left to right and work their way down the page from top to bottom.

Name _____

1.

2.

3.

4.

Phoneme Segmentation
Tell children to listen as you say the word *dot*. Say each sound in the word *dot*, /d//o//t/. Blend the sounds together to say the word /dooot/, *dot*. Explain that there are three sounds in the word. Now say the name of each picture. Then tell children to say the sounds in each picture's name. Encourage them to then count the number of sounds they hear and color in a box for each sound.

Grade K • Unit 4 • Week 2 **173**

Write

Name _____

Dd

1.    _____   d      _____

2.    _____      _____

3.   _____      _____

4. 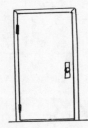   _____      _____

Phonics: /d/d

Point to and say the name of the first picture in the apple row. Explain that it shows a duck. Say: Duck *begins with the /d/ sound.* Explain that the letter *d* stands for the /d/ sound. Now point to and say the names of the rest of the pictures on the page. Have children write the letter *d* next to the picture if its name begins with the /d/ sound as in *duck.* Remind children to look at the pictures in each row from left to right and work their way from the top of the page to the bottom.

174 Grade K • Unit 4 • Week 2

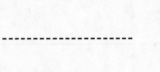
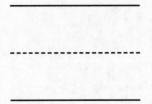

Name _____

Dad dip dim did

1.

_____

- - - - - - - - - - - - - - - - - - - -

_____

2.

_____

- - - - - - - - - - - - - - - - - - - -

_____

3.

_____

- - - - - - - - - - - - - - - - - - - -

_____

Phonics/Spelling
Decode Words: Say *Dan* and point to your mouth position. Write the word and model how to decode it by saying each sound in the name and then blending the sounds together to say the name *Dan*. Then have children decode the words at the top of the page. Spell Words: Have children write the word that names each picture.

Grade K • Unit 4 • Week 2 **175**

Name _____

d

p

c

i

n

Phonics: Letter/Sound Match
Point to the first letter and explain to children that this letter stands for the /d/ sound. Say the name of each picture. Then tell children to draw a line from each letter to the picture whose name begins with that letter. Explain that you will draw a line from the letter *d* to the picture of a dad reading a book because *dad* begins with the /d/ sound spelled *d*.

1.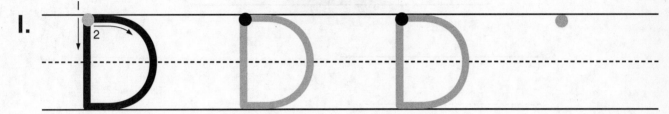

2.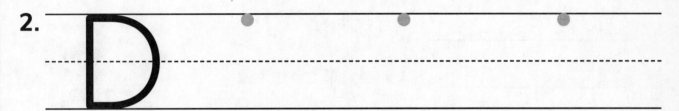

3.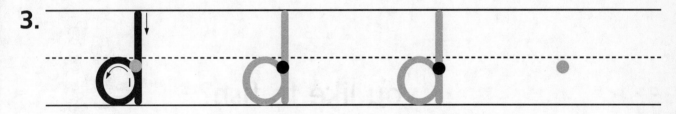

4.

Handwriting *Dd*

Demonstrate to children the proper formation of the uppercase and lowercase letter *Dd*. Say: For the uppercase D, say: *Straight down. Go back to the top. Around and in at the bottom.* For the lowercase d, say: *Circle back and around. Go to the top line. Straight down.* Have children use their finger to trace the model for the letter. Then have them write the uppercase and lowercase forms of the letter *Dd*.

Name _____

do   you

_____
- -

1. I can _____ the laundry.

_____
- - - - - - - - - - - - - - - - - - - -

2. _____ and I can dance.

_____
- -

3. _____ you like to fish?

_____
- - - - - - - - - - - - - - - - - - - -

4. I can _____ the dishes.

High-Frequency Words: *do, you*
Model the Read/Spell/Write routine using the word *do*. Have children repeat the routine. Remind children that the other word in the box is *you*. Tell children to repeat. Have children then write a word from the box on a line to complete each sentence. Have partners read the sentences to each other. Then say the words *do* and *you* for children to spell.

Name _____

1.

 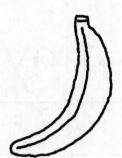 

2.

3.

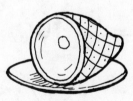  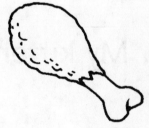

Category Words: Kinds of Foods

Explain to children that there are different kinds of foods. Tell them that an orange, for example, is a type of fruit; string beans are a type of vegetable; a hamburger is a type of meat. Point to and name the pictures in each row. Then have children follow these directions.

1. Circle pictures of vegetables.
2. Circle pictures of fruits.
3. Circle pictures of meats.

big soft tiny sweet

_____

1. We see the _____ jet.

_____

2. Jack sees a _____ ant.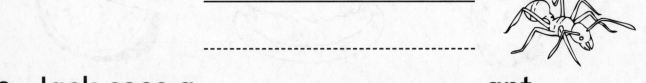

_____

3. My kitten has _____ fur.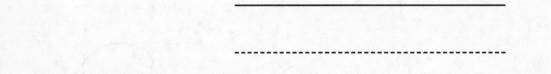

_____

4. I like the _____ orange.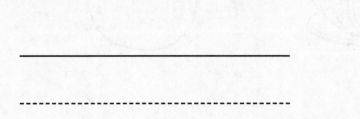

Grammar: Adjectives
Remind children that a adjective describes something or someone. Read the sentences and point to and
name the pictures. Tell children to write a word from the box on the lines to complete each sentence.

1. **My cat climbs the tall tree.**

2. **Nan eats a yellow banana.**

3. **Dan will wash the dirty pan.**

4. **Mom has a soft pillow.**

Grammar: Adjectives
Remind children that a adjective describes something or someone. Read the sentences and point to and name the pictures. Tell children to circle a word in each sentence that is an adjective. Then ask children to refer back to a piece of writing they did during the week and make sure they used adjectives correctly.

1. Do you see Tim.

_____

_____

2. Ican see the dot.

_____

_____

3. Don can d i p the pan.

_____

_____

4. Did Pam See Dan.

_____

_____

Edit/Proofread
Tell children to listen as you read aloud the sentences. Have them rewrite each sentence so it shows correct capitalization and punctuation. Use gestures to clarify meaning.

Name _____

I do!

Connect to Community
Encourage children to read the story to a family member or a friend.

Do You?

Do you like salad ?

Review High-Frequency Words
Have children set a purpose for reading, such as finding out what the bears like to eat. Model pointing from left to right as you read the first sentence of the story. Then ask children to point from left to right as they read the remaining sentences in the story.

Do you like  ?
soup

Do you like  ?
pizza

1.

2.

3.

4.

Phonological Awareness: Identify Rhyme
Remind children that words that rhyme have the same ending sounds. Now point to and say the names of the pictures in each row on the page. Have children circle the two pictures in each row that have names that rhyme.

Name _____

1.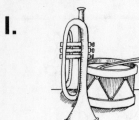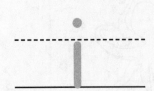

2. 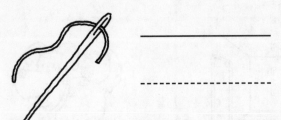 _____ 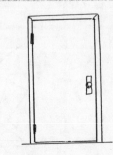 _____

3.  _____  _____

4. 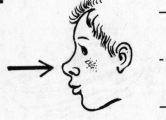 _____   _____

Review Phonics: /i/i, /n/n, /k/c, /o/o, /d/d
Point to and say the word *instruments* in the first row. Say that it begins with the /i/ sound. Explain that the letter *i* stands for the /i/ sound. Now point to and say the names of the rest of the pictures on the page. Have children write the letter that stands for the first sound in the picture name on the lines. Remind children to look at the pictures in each row from left to right and work their way from the top of the page to the bottom.

186 Grade K • Unit 4 • Week 3

Name _____

1.  sn   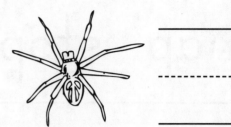 _____

2.  _____    _____

3. 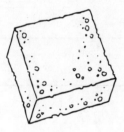 _____    _____

4. 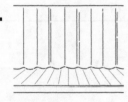 _____    _____

Phonics: Blends *sn, sp, st*

Point to and say the name of the first picture in row I. Say that it shows a snake. Say: *Snake* begins with the sounds /sn/. Point out that the letters *s* and *n* together form the blend *sn*. Now point to and say the names of the rest of the pictures on the page. Have children write the letters *sn, sp,* or *st* for the beginning sounds next to each picture. Remind children to look at the pictures in each row from left to right and work their way from the top of the page to the bottom.

Name _____

snap   stop   spin   spot

1.  _____

2.  _____

3.  _____

Phonics/Spelling

Decode Words: Say *spin*. Write the word and model how to decode it by saying and blending the sounds. Then have children decode the words at the top of the page. Spell Words: Model how to spell *man* and *Stan* by writing a letter for each sound. Then decode the words. Point out to children that they can identify and spell words using the sound-spelling pattern, such as words ending with /an/ as in *man* and *Stan*. Have children write the three picture names using a spelling pattern. Tell children to refer back to a piece of writing and check spelling by using spelling patterns to help them.

Name _____

1. **and**   **go**   **to**

2. **do**   **you**   **and**

3. **go**   **to**   **do**

4. **and**   **you**   **do**

Review High-Frequency Words
Have children follow these directions:

1. Circle the word *go*.   2. Circle the word *you*.
3. Circle the word *to*.   4. Circle the word *do*.

Then say the words *and, do, go, to, you* for children to spell.

Name _____

1.

2.

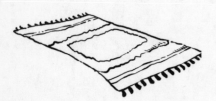  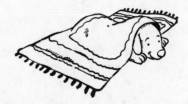

3.

Copyright © McGraw Hill. Permission is granted to reproduce for classroom use.

Category Words: Position Words
Explain to children that the words *up, down, under, over, first,* and *last* tell about positions or where
people or things are. Model by saying *The paper is under my desk,* Point to and name the pictures in each
row. Then have children circle the pictures that show people or animals in certain positions.

190 Grade K • Unit 4 • Week 3

Name _____

I.

2.

  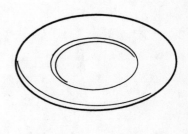

3.

Category Words Review
I. Circle the pictures in this row that show people or animals moving.
2. Circle the pictures in this row that show positions.
3. Circle the pictures in this row that show something happening first and next.

Name _____

fast pretty round small

_____

1. The _____ mouse eats cheese.

_____

----

2. Mom looks at her _____ flowers.

_____

3. The bus has _____ wheels.

_____

4. The _____ train is fun.

Grammar: Adjectives

Remind children that an adjective is a word that describes someone or something. Say: The slow turtle walks by. *The word* slow *describes the turtle.* Point to and say the adjectives in the box. Read the sentences and point to and name the pictures. Help children choose a word from the box to complete each sentence. Have children refer back to a piece of writing and make sure they used adjectives correctly.

1. The round ball is here.

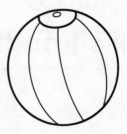

2. I have curly hair.

3. The blue car drives by.

4. The happy baby smiled.

Grammar: Adjectives

Read each sentence and point to and name the pictures. Tell children to draw a line under the word that is an adjective. Then tell children to refer back to a piece of writing that they did during the week and make sure they used adjectives correctly.

1. Tom can sit on themat.

_____

- -

_____

2. Nan can t a p the top of the pot.

_____

- -

_____

3. Sid can sit on the pad

_____

- -

_____

4. i sat at the top.

_____

- -

_____

Edit/Proofread
Tell children to listen as you read aloud the sentences. Have them rewrite each sentence so it shows correct capitalization and punctuation. Use gestures to clarify meaning. Then tell children to refer back to a piece of writing that they did during the week and make sure they used correct capitalization and end punctuation.

Name _____

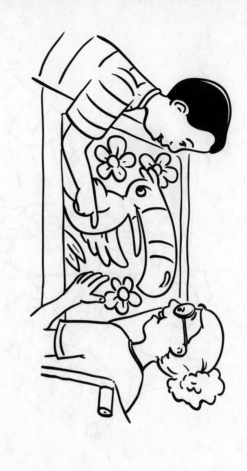

You and I can do it!

Connect to Community
Encourage children to read the story to a family member or a friend.

4

Grade K · Unit 4 · Week 3

You and I

We can go to the park!

Review High-Frequency Words
Have children set a purpose for reading, such as finding out what the children do at the park. Explain that words in a sentence are separated by spaces. Point to the space between the words *go* and *to* on page 1. Then ask children to point to the space between the words *You* and *and* on page 4. Tell children to read from left to right.

1

Can we do it?

We can do a 🧩.
puzzle

Name _____

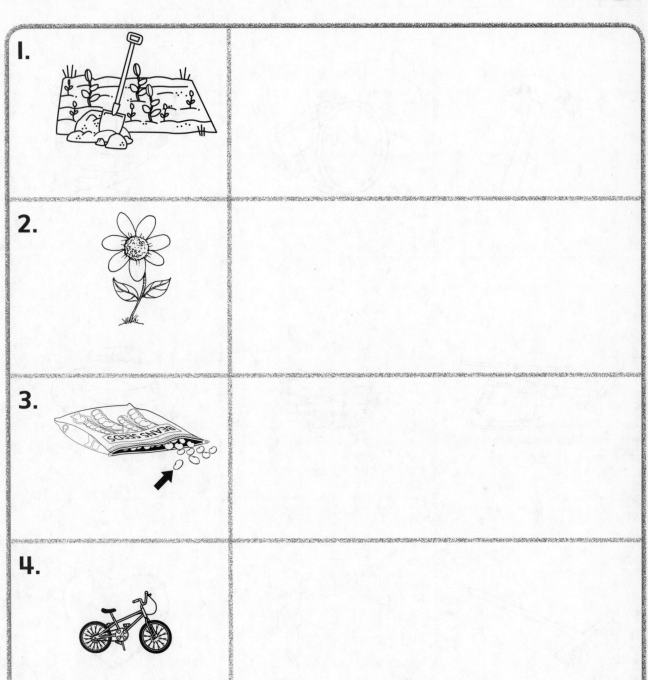

1.

2.

3.

4.

Phonological Awareness: Count and Blend Syllables
Point to a pencil and say its name. Then say each syllable in the word. Model blending the syllables
together to say *pencil*. Model clapping for each syllable in the word. Point out that there are two parts
or syllables in *pencil*. Tell children that you will write the number 2 on the board because *pencil* has two
syllables. Point to and name the remaining pictures. Tell children to say the syllables in each word and
then blend them together to say the whole word. Have them write a number on the line to show how
many parts or syllables they hear.

Phonemic Awareness: /h/
Point to and say the name of the picture of the hammer. Tell children that the word *hammer* begins with the /h/ sound. Have children repeat, *hammer, /h/*. Now point to and say the names of the rest of the pictures on the page. Tell children to circle the pictures that have names that begin with the /h/ sound as in *hammer*. Tell children to look at the pictures in each row from left to right and work their way down the page from top to bottom.

1.

2.

3.

4.

Phonemic Awareness: Phoneme Categorization
Point to and say the name of the pictures on the page. Tell children to circle the two pictures in each row that have names that begin with the /h/ sound as in *hut*. Tell children to look at the pictures in each row from left to right and work their way down the page from top to bottom.

Write

Name _____

Hh

1.

h

2.

3.

4.

Phonics: /h/h
Point to and say the name of the picture of the hat. Tell children that the word *hat* begins with the /h/ sound. Explain that the letter *h* stands for the /h/ sound. Now point to and say the names of the rest of the pictures on the page. Have children write the letter *h* next to the picture if its name begins with /h/ sound as in *hat*. Tell children to look at the pictures in each row from left to right. Then tell them to work their way from the top of the page to the bottom.

Stan spin hot hid

1.

2.

3.

Phonics/Spelling

Decode Words: Say *had* and point to your mouth position. Model how to spell the word *had* by writing a letter for each sound you hear. Then decode the word. Then have children decode the words at the top of the page. Spell Words: Have children write the word that names each picture on the lines.

Name _____

h

sn

o

st

i

Phonics: Letter/Sound Match
Point to the first letter and explain to children that this letter stands for the /h/ sound. Say the name of each picture. Then tell children to draw a line from each letter to the picture whose name begins with that letter.

Name _____

Hh

1.

2.

3.

4.

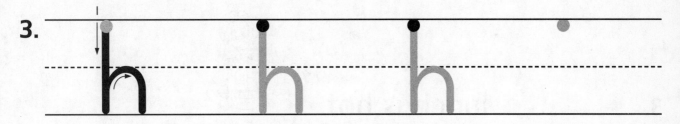

Handwriting: *Hh*
Demonstrate to children the proper formation of the uppercase and lowercase *Hh*. For the uppercase H, say: *Straight down. Go back to the top. Straight down. Straight across the dotted line.* For the lowercase h, say: *Straight down. Go to the dotted line. Around and down.* Tell children to use their finger to trace the model for the letter. Then have them write the uppercase and lowercase forms of the letter *Hh*.

my   you

_____
- - - - - - - - - - - - - - - -

1. I can do _____ work.

_____
- - - - - - - - - - - - - - - -

2. _____ give the plants water.

_____
- - - - - - - - - - - - - - - -

3. _____ lunch is hot.

_____
- - - - - - - - - - - - - - - -

4. I can put away _____ toys.

High-Frequency Words: *my, you*
Model the Read/Spell/Write routine using the word *my*. Have children repeat the routine. Remind children that the other word in the box is *you*. Tell children to repeat. Have children then write a word from the box on a line to complete each sentence. Have partners read the sentences to each other. Then say the words *my* and *you* aloud for children to spell.

Name _____

1.

2.

3.

Category Words: Size Words
Explain to children that people and animals can be different sizes. Tell children that some of the pictures on this page show animals and things that are small or big, as well as short and tall. Point to and name the pictures in each row. Have children circle the two pictures in each row that show something small and big.

Grade K • Unit 5 • Week 1 **205**

Name _____

_____

----

1. _____ plays soccer.

   She   He

2. _____ paints.

   He   She

3. _____ plays the piano.

   We   She

Grammar: Subjective Pronouns
Explain to children that a pronoun takes the place of someone's name or a noun. Tell them that the word *he* takes the place of *the boy*. Instead of saying *The boy reads*, we can say *He reads*. Then read each example and point to and name the pictures. Tell children to circle the pronoun that best completes each sentence.

206 Grade K • Unit 5 • Week 1

Name _____

| He | She | It | We |

_____

1. _____ sails by.

_____

2. _____ is tall.

_____

3. _____ cooks.

_____

4. _____ can color.

Grammar: Subjective Pronouns
Remind children that a pronoun takes the place of someone's name or a noun. Read the sentences and point to and name the pictures. Tell children to write a pronoun from the box on the lines to complete each sentence. Then tell children to refer back to a piece of writing that they did during the week and make sure they used pronouns correctly.

1. We like to go to the t o p.

_____

- -

_____

2. sid hid the pan.

_____

- -

_____

3. We like to mop

_____

- -

_____

4. we go to the garden.

_____

- -

_____

Edit/Proofread
Tell children to listen as you read aloud the sentences. Have them rewrite each sentence so it shows correct capitalization and punctuation. Use gestures to clarify meaning. Tell children to refer back to a piece of writing that they did during the week and make sure they used correct capitalization and end punctuation.

We do not see my cat.

Connect to Community

Encourage children to read the story to a family member or a friend.

4

We See It!

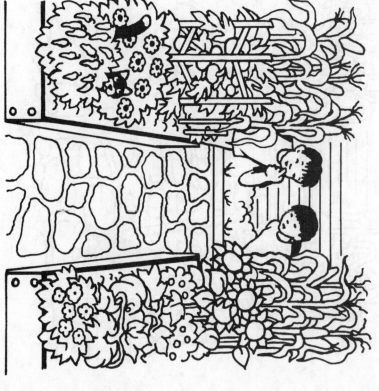

Tam and I see my cat.

Review High-Frequency Words

Have children set a purpose for reading, such as finding out what the children see. Tell children that a word is made up of letters. Point to the first and last letters in the word see and the space between see and my. Then ask children to point to the first and last letters in *and* and the space between *and* and *I*.

1

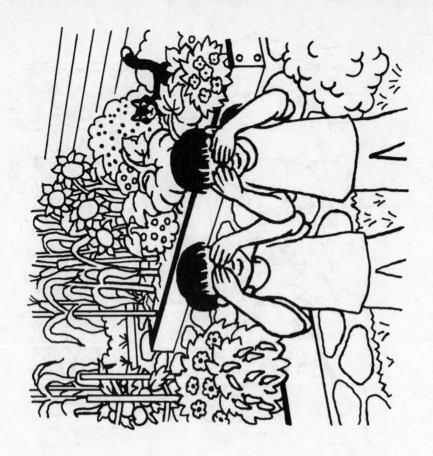

Tam and I do not see.

My cat and I see Tam.

Draw

1.	2.
3.	4.

Phonological Awareness: Onset and Rime Blending
Say the word *met*. Then say /m/ /et/, *met*. Have children repeat. Explain that you first said the beginning sound in the word *met* and then you said the remaining sounds. Say that you blended the sounds together to say *met*. Tell children that you will say the beginning and ending sounds in some words. Have them blend the sounds together to say the word. Then tell children to draw a picture of the word in each box. l. /p//en/, *pen*; 2. /t//en/, *ten*; 3. /m//en/, *men*; 4. /p//et/, *pet*.

Phonemic Awareness: /e/

Point to and say the name of the picture of the envelope. Tell children that the word *envelope* begins with the /e/ sound. Have children repeat, *envelope*, /e/. Now point to and say the names of the rest of the pictures on the page. Tell children to circle the pictures that have names that begin with the /e/ sound as in *envelope*. Tell children to look at the pictures in each row from left to right and work their way down the page from top to bottom.

Name _____

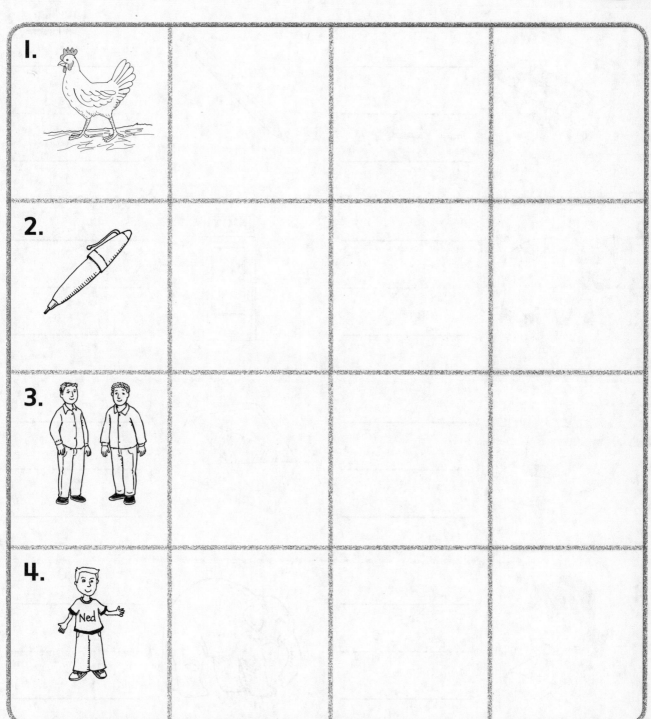

1.

2.

3.

4.

Phonemic Awareness: Phoneme Segmentation

Tell children to listen as you say the word *ten*. Say each sound in the word *ten*, /t//e//n/. Then blend the sounds together to say the word *ten*. Explain that there are three sounds in the word. Now say the name of each picture. Then tell children to say the sounds in each picture's name. Encourage them to then count the number of sounds they hear and color in a box for each sound.

1.

e

2.

EXIT

3.

4.

Phonics: /e/ e

Point to and say the name of the picture of the eggs. Tell children that the word *eggs* begins with the /e/ sound. Explain that the letter *e* stands for the /e/ sound. Now point to and say the names of the rest of the pictures on the page. Have children write the letter *e* next to the picture if its name begins with /e/ sound as in *eggs*. Tell children to look at the pictures in each row from left to right. Then tell them to work their way from the top of the page to the bottom.

Name _____

den pet met set

1.

_____

- -

_____

2.

_____

- -

_____

3.

_____

- -

_____

4.

_____

- -

_____

Phonics/Spelling

Decode Words: Say *Ted* and point to your mouth position. Write *Ted* and model how to decode it. Have children decode the words at the top of the page. Spell Words: Model how to spell *hen* by writing a letter for each sound. Point out that every word needs to have a vowel, such as the *e* in *hen*. Write and decode the word. Have children write the word that names each picture by writing a letter for each sound. Point out the spelling rule that each word needs to have a vowel. Then have children refer back to a piece of writing and check that they included a vowel in each word.

Draw

Name _____

e

sn

h

st

o

Phonics: Letter/Sound Match
Point to the first letter and explain to children that this letter stands for the /e/ sound. Say the name of each picture. Then tell children to draw a line from each letter to the picture whose name begins with that letter.

216 Grade K • Unit 5 • Week 2

Name _____

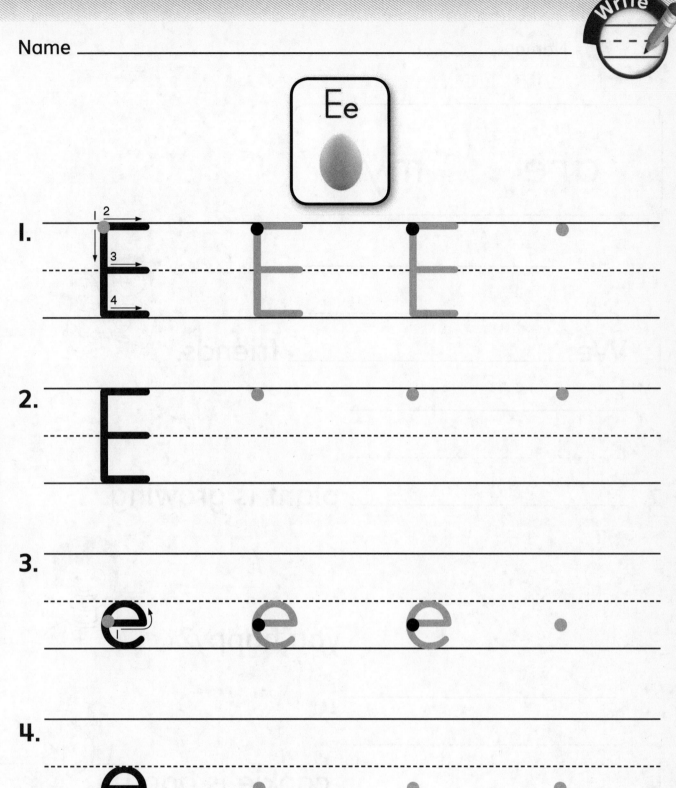

1.

2.

3.

4.

Handwriting: *Ee*

Demonstrate to children the proper formation of the uppercase and lowercase *Ee*. For the uppercase
E, say: *Straight down. Straight across. Straight across. Straight across.* For the lowercase e, say: *Straight
across. Circle back and around, then stop.* Have children use their finger to trace the model for the letter.
Repeat with modeling the proper formation of the uppercase and lowercase *Ee*. Then have them write the
uppercase and lowercase forms of the letter *Ee*.

Grade K • Unit 5 • Week 2 **217**

are   my

_____
- -

1. We _____ friends.

_____
- -

2. _____ plant is growing.

_____
- -

3. _____ you happy?

_____
- -

4. _____ cookie is good.

High-Frequency Words: *are, my*
Model the Read/Spell/Write routine using the word *are*. Have children repeat the routine. Remind children that the other word in the box is *my*. Tell children to repeat. Have children then write a word from the box on a line to complete each sentence. Have partners read the sentences to each other. Say the words *are* and *my* for children to spell.

Name _____

1.

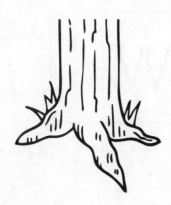  

2.

3.

Category Words: Tree Parts
Explain to children that trees have different parts. Tell children that some of the pictures on this page show parts of trees. Point to and name the pictures in each row. Have children circle the two pictures in each row that show parts of trees.

Name _____

He She It We

_____

1. _____ sails by.

2. _____ is tall.

3. _____ cooks.

4. _____ are flying kites.

Grammar: Subjective Pronouns
Remind children that a pronoun takes the place of someone's name or a noun. Tell them that the word *they* takes the place of *The mother and father*. Instead of saying *The mother and father are proud*, I can say *They are proud*. Then read each example and point to and name the pictures. Tell children to write the pronoun that completes each sentence.

_____

----

1. _____ rides a red bike.

He   We

_____

----

2. _____ jumps rope.

It   She

_____

----

3. _____ write a story.

They   She

Grammar: Subjective Pronouns
Remind children that a pronoun takes the place of someone's name or a noun. Say: *Listen to this sentence:*
The boy went to school. *Now listen to this sentence:* He went to school. *The word* He *takes the place of*
The boy. He *is a pronoun.* Then read each example and point to and name the pictures. Tell children to
write the pronoun that completes each sentence. Tell children to refer back to a piece of writing that they
did during the week and make sure that they used pronouns correctly.

1. Can ted see you?

_____

_____

2. Can I see the pet?

_____

_____

3. they can see the trees.

_____

_____

Edit/Proofread

Tell children to listen as you read the sentences. Remind children that a sentence begins with a capital letter and has end punctuation, such as a period. Explain that a person's name also begins with a capital letter. Have them rewrite each sentence so it shows correct capitalization and punctuation. Then have children refer back to a piece of writing they did during the week to be sure they used a capital letter for the first letter in a sentence and in a person's name. Model using the Read/Spell/Write routine to spell *are*, and have children use the routine to check the high-frequency words they used.

Name _____

We are not sad.

We can hop!

Connect to Community
Encourage children to read the story to a family member or a friend.

Grade K • Unit 5 • Week 2

Copyright © McGraw Hill

Are You Hot?

Are you hot?

Are you sad?

Review High-Frequency Words
Have children set a purpose for reading, such as finding out what the children do to feel cooler. Explain that words in a sentence are separated by spaces. Point to the space between the words Are and you on page 1. Then ask children to point to the space between the words are and not on page 4.

1

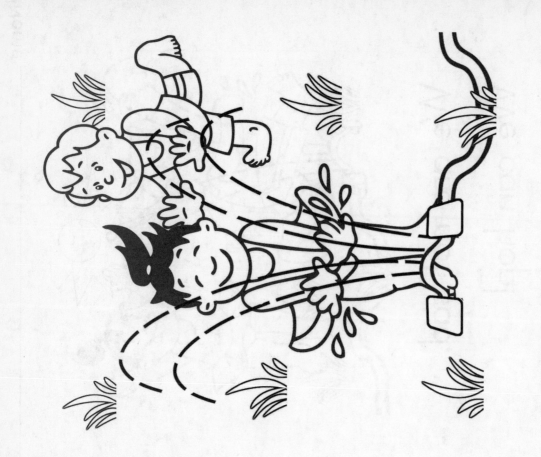

We are not hot.

We can go!

Name _____

1.

2.

3.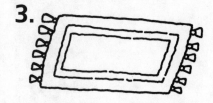

4.

Phonological Awareness: Identify Rhyme
Remind children that words that rhyme have the same ending sounds. Now point to and say the names of the pictures in each row on the page. Have children circle the two pictures in each row that have names that rhyme.

Phonemic Awareness: /f/

Point to and say the name of the picture of the fan. Tell children that the word *fan* begins with the /f/ sound. Have children repeat, *fan*, /f/. Now point to and say the names of the rest of the pictures on the page. Tell children to circle the pictures that have names that begin with the /f/ sound as in *fan*. Tell children to look at the pictures in each row from left to right and work their way down the page from top to bottom.

Phonemic Awareness: /r/

Point to and say the name of the picture of the rug. Tell children that the word *rug* begins with the /r/ sound. Have children repeat, *rug*, /r/. Now point to and say the names of the rest of the pictures on the page. Tell children to circle the pictures that have names that begin with the /r/ sound as in *rug*. Tell children to look at the pictures in each row from left to right and work their way down the page from top to bottom.

1.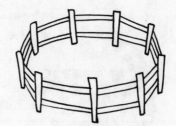

2.

3.

4.

Phonemic Awareness: Phoneme Addition

Say *an*. Then add /p/ to the beginning of *an* to form *pan*. Point out that the word *pan* was formed after a sound was added to the beginning of *an*. Name the pictures in each row. Tell children to circle the picture in each row that is formed after you say the following: Row 1: Add /f/ to *an*; Row 2: Add /h/ to *am*; Row 3: Add /p/ to *in*; Row 4: Add /b/ to *at*.

Name _____

1.

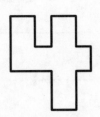

- - - - f - - - - - - - -

_____

- - - - - - - - - - - - -

_____

2.

- - - - - - - - - - - - -

_____

- - - - - - - - - - - - -

_____

3.

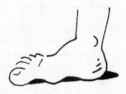

- - - - - - - - - - - - -

_____

- - - - - - - - - - - - -

_____

4.

- - - - - - - - - - - - -

_____

- - - - - - - - - - - - -

_____

Phonics: /f/f

Point to and say the name of the picture of the number four. Tell children that the word *four* begins with the /f/ sound. Explain that the letter *f* stands for the /f/ sound. Now point to and say the name of the rest of the pictures on the page. Have children write the letter *f* next to the picture if its name begins with the /f/ sound as in *four*. Tell children to look at the pictures in each row from left to right. Then tell them to work their way from the top of the page to the bottom.

Grade K • Unit 5 • Week 3 **229**

Name _____

Rr

1.    ------ r ------

2. 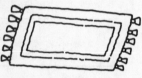   ------------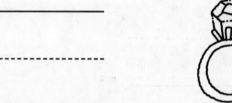

3.    ------------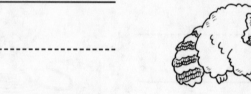

4. 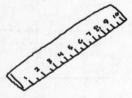   ------------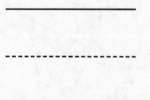

Phonics: /r/r
Point to and say the name of the picture of the rose. Tell children that the word *rose* begins with the /r/ sound. Explain that the letter *r* stands for the /r/ sound. Now point to and say the names of the rest of the pictures on the page. Have children write the letter *r* next to the picture if its name begins with /r/ sound as in *rose*. Tell children to look at the pictures in each row from left to right. Then tell them to work their way from the top of the page to the bottom.

230 Grade K • Unit 5 • Week 3

Name _____

if   rim   fed   red

1.

_____

- - - - - - - - - - - - - - - - - - -

_____

2.

_____

- - - - - - - - - - - - - - - - - - -

_____

3.

_____

- - - - - - - - - - - - - - - - - - -

_____

4.

_____

- - - - - - - - - - - - - - - - - - -

_____

Phonics/Spelling

Decode Words: Say *it* and point to your mouth position. Write the word and model how to decode it by saying the sound for each letter in the word and then blending the sounds together to say *it*. Then say *ran* and point to your mouth position. Have children decode the words at the top of the page. Spell Words: Model how to spell the word *rip* by writing a letter for each sound. Point out that every word needs to have a vowel, such as the *i* in *rip*. Then decode the word. Have children write the word that names each picture by writing a letter for each sound. Remind children that each word needs to have a vowel.

Name _____

1. **fan**   **in**   **fin**

2. **fit**   **fed**   **pit**

3. **rod**   **red**   **ram**

4. **rid**   **rip**   **rap**

5. **if**   **fit**   **in**

Phonics: Minimal Contrasts
Tell children that when you change one letter in a word, you make a new word. Write the words *fan* and
fin. Explain that by changing the a in *fan* to an *i*, you make the word *fin*. Have children read the first word
in each row. Tell them to draw a line under the new word that is formed when one letter in the word
is changed. Then say the words *if, it,* and *in* for children to spell.

Name _____

1.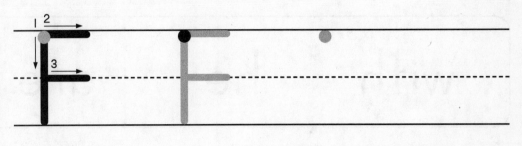

2.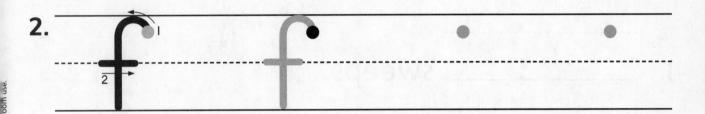

3.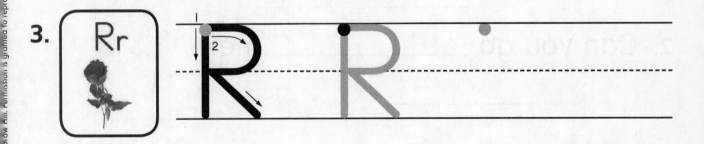

4.

Handwriting: *Ff, Rr*
Demonstrate to children the proper formation of the uppercase and lowercase *Ff*. For the uppercase F, say: *Straight down. Straight across. Straight across.* For the lowercase f, say: *Circle back a little, then straight down. Go to the dotted line. Straight across.* Demonstrate the proper formation of the uppercase and lowercase *Rr*. For the uppercase R, say: *Straight down. Go back to the top. Around and in at the dotted line. Slant down.* For the lowercase r, say: *Straight down. Curl forward.* Have children use their finger to trace the model for each letter. Then have them write the uppercase and lowercase forms of the letters *Ff* and *Rr*.

with	he	are

_____

----

1. _____ sweeps.

_____

----

2. Can you go _____ me?

_____

----

3. We _____ eating.

_____

----

4. _____

High-Frequency Words: *with*, *he*, *are*
Model the Read/Spell/Write routine using the word *with*. Have children repeat the routine. Repeat the routine with the word *he*. Remind children that the other word in the box is *are*. Tell children to repeat. Have children then write a word from the box on a line to complete each sentence. Encourage children to then write their own sentence using one or more of the words. Have partners read the sentences to each other. Then say the words *with*, *he*, and *are* for children to spell.

Name _____

1.

2.

 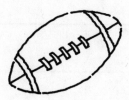 

3.

Category Words: Foods
Explain to children that people and animals eat different kinds of food to stay healthy. Tell children that some of the pictures on this page show different foods. Point to and name the pictures in each row. Have children circle the two pictures in each row that show foods. Encourage pairs of children to use the food words in sentences.

He She They I

_____

1. _____ skate.

_____

2. _____ sleeps.

_____

3. _____ draws.

_____

4. _____

Grammar: Subjective Pronouns
Remind children that a pronoun takes the place of a noun. Read the sentences and point to and name the pictures. Tell children to write a pronoun from the box on the lines to complete each sentence. Then tell children to write a sentence using one or more of the words in the box. Have children refer to a piece of writing that they did during the week and make sure they used pronouns correctly.

Name _____

_____

_____

1. _____ like to sing.

She   We

_____

_____

2. _____ can dance.

They   She

_____

_____

3. _____ needs water.

It   He

Grammar: Subjective Pronouns
Remind children that a pronoun takes the place of a noun. Then read each example and point to and
name the pictures. Tell children to write the pronoun that best completes each sentence.

1. Can we fit!

_____

_____

2. I see a fat hen

_____

_____

3. Did sid pet the cat?

_____

_____

4. we are with the cat.

_____

_____

Edit/Proofread

Tell children to listen as you read aloud the sentences. Have them rewrite each sentence so it shows correct capitalization and punctuation. Explain to children that the first letter in a sentence and in person's name should always be a capital letter. Then tell children to refer back to a piece of writing they did during the week and check that they used correct capitalization and end punctuation. Remind children to make sure they capitalized the first letter in a sentence and in a person's name.

He sat with mom.

Mom fed him!

Connect to Community
Encourage children to read the story to a family member or a friend.

Tim

He fed the hen.

He sat with the cat.

Review High-Frequency Words
Have children set a purpose for reading, such as finding out what Tim did. Explain that words are made up of letters. Say: *The word with has four letters:* w, i, t, *and* h. Have children point to the word *he* on page 1 and tell how many letters are in the word. Then explain to children that when they get to the end of a line, they look at the first word in the next line and continue to read from left to right. Model these concepts of print for children.

He sat with Nat.

He fed the cat.

Name _____

1.	**2.**
3.	**4.**

Phonological Awareness: Onset and Rime Segmentation
Remind children that words are made up of beginning and ending sounds. Say the word *bin*. Tell children that the beginning sound is /b/. Then say that the ending sounds are /iiinnn/, *in*. Tell children to say the word, *bin*. Then say some words and encourage children to say the beginning and ending sounds in each word. Have children draw a picture in each box that shows the word. I. *lap*, /l//ap/, lap; 2. *bat*, /b//at/, bat; 3. *bin*, /b//in/, bin; 4. *lip*, /l/ /ip/, lip.

Phonemic Awareness: /b/

Point to and say the name of the picture of the box. Tell children that the word *box* begins with the /b/ sound. Have children repeat, *box*, /b/. Now point to and say the names of the rest of the pictures on the page. Tell children to circle the pictures that have names that begin with the /b/ sound as in *box*. Tell children to look at the pictures in each row from left to right and work their way down the page from top to bottom.

242 Grade K • Unit 6 • Week 1

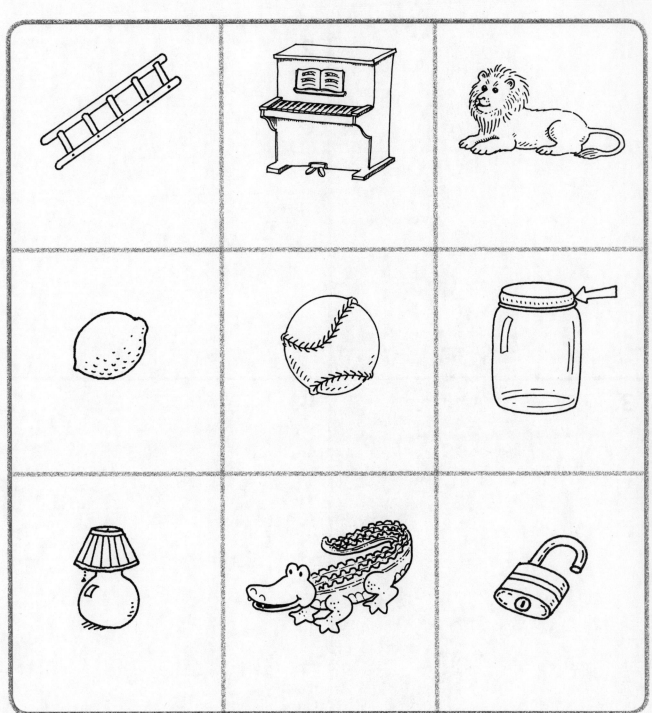

Phonemic Awareness: /l/

Point to and say the name of the picture of the ladder. Tell children that the word *ladder* begins with the /l/ sound. Have children repeat, *ladder*, /l/. Now point to and say the names of the rest of the pictures on the page. Tell children to circle the pictures that have names that begin with the /l/ sound as in *ladder*. Tell children to look at the pictures in each row from left to right and work their way down the page from top to bottom.

1.

2.

3.

4.

Phonemic Awareness: Phoneme Blending with /b/, /l/
Tell children to listen to the sounds in the word *bit*. Model blending the sounds to say the word *bit*, /biiit/,
bit. Have children repeat. Then model blending the sounds to say the word *lid*, /llliiid/, lid. Tell children you
will say the sounds in more words. Have them blend the sounds to say each word. Then have them draw a
picture of the word: 1. /b//e//d/; 2. /l//i//p/; 3. /l//a//b/; 4. /b//a//t/.

Bb

Name _____

I.  _____ b _____  _____

2.  _____ _____  _____ _____

3.  _____ _____  _____ _____

4.  _____ _____  _____ _____

Phonics: /b/ b

Point to and say the name of the picture of the bib. Tell children that the word *bib* begins with the /b/ sound. Explain that the letter *b* stands for the /b/ sound. Now point to and say the names of the rest of the pictures on the page. Have children write the letter *b* next to the picture if its name begins with /b/ sound as in *bib*. Tell children to look at the pictures in each row from left to right. Then tell them to work their way from the top of the page to the bottom.

Ll

1.

_____

- - - - - | - - - - -

_____

_____

- - - - - - - - -

_____

2.

_____

- - - - - - - - -

_____

_____

- - - - - - - - -

_____

3.

_____

- - - - - - - - -

_____

_____

- - - - - - - - -

_____

4.

_____

- - - - - - - - -

_____

_____

- - - - - - - - -

_____

Phonics: /l/
Point to and say the name of the picture of the ladder. Tell children that the word *ladder* begins with the /l/ sound. Explain that the letter *l* stands for the /l/ sound. Now point to and say the names of the rest of the pictures on the page. Have children write the letter *l* next to the picture if its name begins with /l/ sound as in *ladder*. Tell children to look at the pictures in each row from left to right. Then tell them to work their way from the top of the page to the bottom.

Name _____

bad   led   lit   bet

1.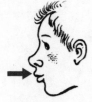
_____
- -
_____

2.
_____
- -
_____

3.
_____
- -
_____

4.
_____
- -
_____

Phonics/Spelling
Decode Words: Say *lap* and point to your mouth position. Write the word and model how to decode it by saying the sound for each letter in the word and then blending the sounds together to say *lap*. Then repeat with the name *Bob*. Have children decode the words at the top of the page. Spell Words: Have children write the word that names each picture.

Name _____

1. **lot**   **lid**   **lit**

2. **bit**   **bat**   **fat**

3. **rib**   **rob**   **red**

4. **rid**   **red**   **Ron**

5. **bed**   **bin**   **bad**

Phonics: Minimal Contrasts
Tell children that when you change one letter in a word, you make a new word. Write the words *Deb* and *den*. Explain that by changing the *b* in *Deb* to an *n*, you make the word *den*. Have children read the first word in each row. Tell them to draw a line under the new word that is formed when one letter in the word is changed.

Name _____

1. Bb

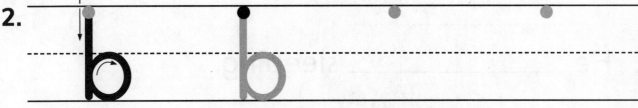

2.

3. Ll

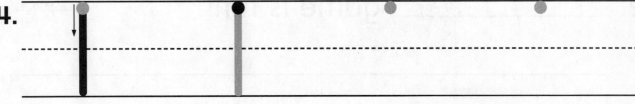

4.

Handwriting: *Bb, Ll*
Model for children how to form the uppercase letter *B. Straight down. Go back to the top. Around and in, around and in.* Model how the lowercase *b* is formed. *Straight down. Go to the dotted line. Around all the way.* Model how to form the uppercase letter *L. Straight down. Straight across the bottom line.* Then model how to form the lowercase *l. Straight down.* Have children use their finger to trace the model for each letter. Then have them write the uppercase and lowercase forms of the letters *Bb* and *Ll*.

is   little   my

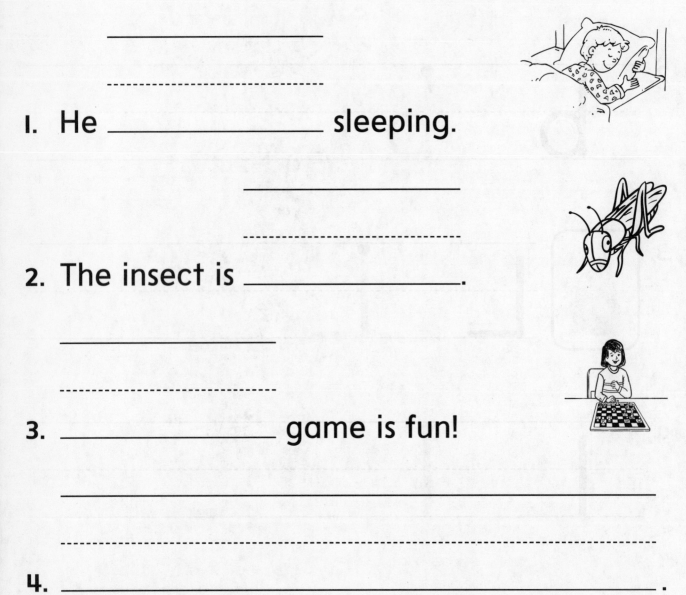

_____

- - - - - - - - - - - - - - - -

1. He _____ sleeping.

_____

- - - - - - - - - - - - - - - -

2. The insect is _____ .

_____

- - - - - - - - - - - - - -

3. _____ game is fun!

_____

- -

4. _____ .

High-Frequency Words: *is, little, my*
Model the Read/Spell/Write routine using the word *is*. Have children repeat the routine. Repeat the routine with the word *little*. Remind children that the other word in the box is *my*. Tell children to repeat. Have children then write a word from the box on a line to complete each sentence. Encourage children to then write their own sentence using one or more of the words. Have partners read the sentences to each other. Then say the words *is, little, and my* for children to spell.

Name _____

I.

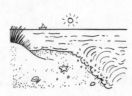  

2.

3.

Category Words: Seasons
Explain to children that there are different seasons. Winter is usually cold and snowy. The leaves turn colors in the fall. Tell children that some of the pictures on this page show seasonal things or things you do during different seasons. Point to and name the pictures in each row. Have children circle the two pictures in each row that show something about seasons.

1. Rob can see the _____.

               hen   hens

2. Nan had a _____.

               bat   bats

3. Ed had _____.

               cat   cats

Grammar: Plural Nouns
Explain to children that some nouns name one thing and some name more than one thing. Then read each example and point to and name the pictures. Help children read the two word choices for each example and write the singular or plural noun that completes each sentence.Tell children to refer back to a piece of writing that they did during the week and check to make sure they used plural nouns correctly. Tell them to also use spelling patterns to help them as they write and to also make sure they spelled high-frequency words correctly.

Name _____

_____
----

1. Can you see the _____?

fox   foxes

_____
----

2. The _____ are hot.

pan   pans

_____
----

3. The _____ are little.

boxes   box

Grammar: Plural Nouns
Remind children that some nouns name one thing and some name more than one thing. Then read each example and the two answer choices. Point to and name the pictures. Help children write the plural noun that completes each sentence.

I. Wedo not see it.

_____

_____

2. Can he go with us!

_____

_____

3. We can go with Rob?

_____

_____

4. go with her to school.

_____

_____

Edit/Proofread
Tell children to listen as you read aloud the sentences. Have them rewrite each sentence so it shows correct capitalization and punctuation. Use gestures to clarify meaning. Then tell children to refer back to a piece of writing they did during the week and check that they used correct capitalization and end punctuation. Encourage them to use spelling patterns to help them write and to check that they spelled high-frequency words correctly.

Deb can sit on it!

It is big!

Connect to Community
Encourage children to read the story to a family member or a friend.

Little and Big

Deb can see it.

It is little.

Review High-Frequency Words
Have children set a purpose for reading, such as finding out what is little and big. Explain that words in a sentence are separated by spaces. Point to the space between the words *is* and *little* on page 1. Have children then point to the words *is* and *not* on page 3. Then ask them to point to where they will continue reading after they get to the end of the line.

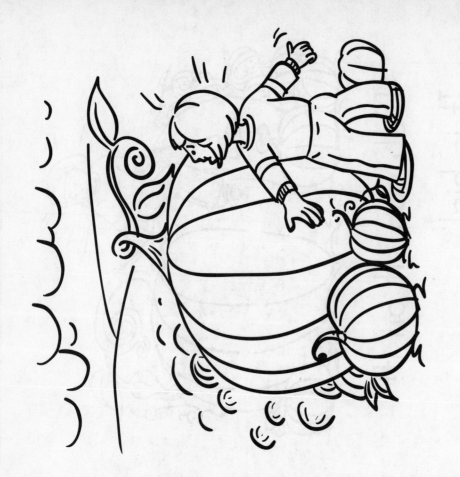

It is not little.

Deb can pat it in.

Name _____

1.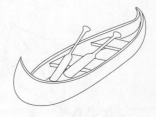

2.

3.

4.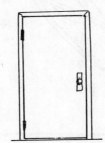

Phonological Awareness: Identify Rhyme
Remind children that words that rhyme have the same ending sounds. Now point to and say the names of the pictures in each row on the page. Have children circle the two pictures in each row that have names that rhyme.

Phonemic Awareness: /k/

Point to and say the name of the picture of the kite. Tell children that the word *kite* begins with the /k/ sound. Have children repeat, *kite*, /k/. Now point to and say the names of the rest of the pictures on the page. Tell children to circle the pictures that have names that begin with the /k/ sound as in *kite*. Tell children to look at the pictures in each row from left to right and work their way down the page from top to bottom.

Name _____

Phonemic Awareness: /k/, /ck/
Point to and say the name of the picture of the giraffe kicking. Tell children that *kick* begins and ends with the /k/ sound. Now point to and say the names of the pictures on the page. Tell children to circle the pictures that have names that end with the /k/ sound. Tell children to look at the pictures in each row from left to right and work their way down the page from top to bottom.

Grade K • Unit 6 • Week 2 **259**

Name _____

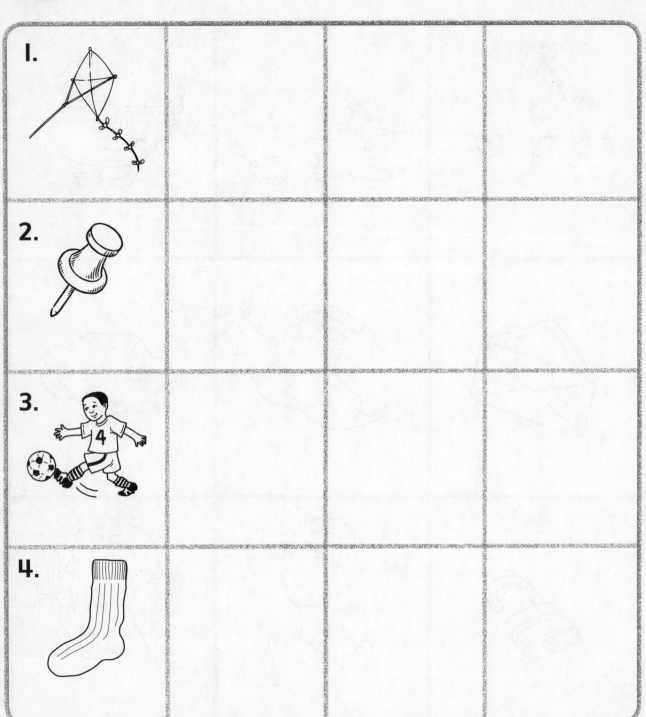

1.

2.

3.

4.

Phonemic Awareness: Phoneme Segmentation

Tell children to listen as you say the word *kit*. Say each sound in the word *kit*, /k//i//t/. Then blend the sounds together to say the word *kit*. Explain that there are three sounds in the word. Now say the name of each picture. Then tell children to say the sounds in each picture's name. Encourage them to count the number of sounds they hear and color in a box for each sound.

Kk

Name _____

1.  ‾‾‾‾‾‾‾‾‾‾‾‾‾‾‾‾
k ‾ ‾ ‾ ‾ ‾ ‾ ‾ ‾ ‾ ‾
_____ 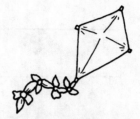 ‾‾‾‾‾‾‾‾‾‾‾‾‾‾‾‾
- - - - - - - - - - - - - - - -
_____

2.  ‾‾‾‾‾‾‾‾‾‾‾‾‾‾‾‾
- - - - - - - - - - - - - - - -
_____  ‾‾‾‾‾‾‾‾‾‾‾‾‾‾‾‾
- - - - - - - - - - - - - - - -
_____

3.  ‾‾‾‾‾‾‾‾‾‾‾‾‾‾‾‾
- - - - - - - - - - - - - - - -
_____  ‾‾‾‾‾‾‾‾‾‾‾‾‾‾‾‾
- - - - - - - - - - - - - - - -
_____

4.  ‾‾‾‾‾‾‾‾‾‾‾‾‾‾‾‾
- - - - - - - - - - - - - - - -
_____  ‾‾‾‾‾‾‾‾‾‾‾‾‾‾‾‾
- - - - - - - - - - - - - - - -
_____

Phonics: /k/ k
Point to and say the name of the picture of the key. Tell children that the word *key* begins with the /k/ sound. Explain that the letter *k* stands for the /k/ sound. Now point to and say the name of the rest of the pictures on the page. Have children write the letter *k* next to the picture if its name begins with the /k/ sound as in *key*. Tell children to look at the pictures in each row from left to right. Then tell them to work their way from the top of the page to the bottom.

I.

$- - - -$ ck

2.

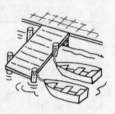

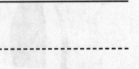

3.

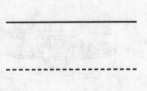

4.

Phonics: /k/ *ck*

Point to and say the name of the picture of the tack. Tell children that the word *tack* ends with the /k/ sound spelled *ck*. Now point to and say the names of the rest of the pictures on the page. Have children write the letters *ck* next to the picture if its name ends with the /k/ sound as in *tack*. Tell children to look at the pictures in each row from left to right. Then tell them to work their way from the top of the page to the bottom.

Name _____

Kim deck rack kit

1.

_____

- -

_____

2.

_____

- -

_____

3.

_____

- -

_____

4.

_____

- -

_____

Phonics/Spelling

Decode Words: Say *Kim* and point to your mouth position. Write the word and model how to decode it. Then repeat with the word *speck*. Have children decode the words at the top of the page by saying each of the sounds in the name and then blending them together to say *Kim*. Spell Words: Then have them write the word that names each picture.

1. **Kim**   **lick**   **kit**

2. **sick**   **sock**   **snack**

3. **duck**   **deck**   **rock**

4. **kid**   **sack**   **kit**

5. **stack**   **speck**   **stick**

Phonics: Minimal Contrasts
Tell children that when you change one letter in a word, you make a new word. Write the words *Kim* and *kit*. Explain that by changing the *m* in *Kim* to a *t*, you make the word *kit*. Have children read the first word in each row. Tell them to draw a line under the new word that is formed when one letter in the word is changed. Then write the words *lick, lock, sock,* and *dock* on the board and have children decode them.

Name _____

Kk

1. K K

2. k k

3. ck ck

4. ck

Handwriting: *Kk*

Model for children how to form the uppercase *K*. *Straight down. Go back to the top. Slant in, slant out.*
Model how the lowercase *k* is formed. *Straight down. Slant in, slant out.* Remind children how to form the
uppercase and lowercase *c*. Have children use their finger to trace the model for the letter. Then have
them write the uppercase and lowercase forms of the letters *Kk*. Repeat for the lowercase forms of the
letters *ck*.

Name _____

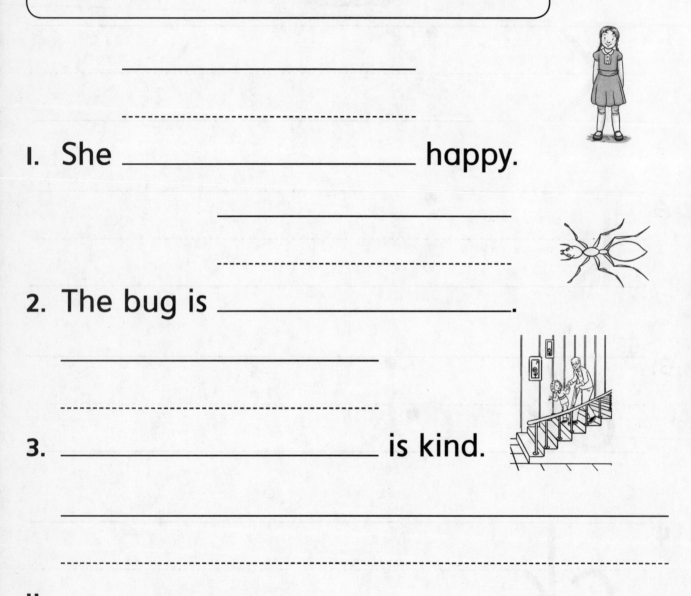

she   was   little

_____

- -

1. She _____ happy.

- -

2. The bug is _____.

- -

3. _____ is kind.

_____

- -

4. _____

High-Frequency Words: *she, was, little*
Model the Read/Spell/Write routine using the word *she*. Have children repeat the routine. Repeat with the word *was*. Remind children that the other word in the box is *little*. Tell children to repeat. Have children then write a word from the box on a line to complete each sentence. Encourage children to then write their own sentence using one or more of the words. Have partners read the sentences to each other. Say the words *she*, *was*, and *little* for children to spell.

Name _____

I.

2.

  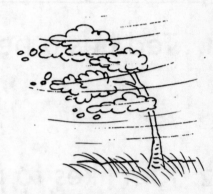

3.

Category Words: Weather Words
Explain to children that there are different kinds of weather, such as sunny, rainy, stormy. Tell children that some of the pictures on this page show different weather conditions. Point to and name the pictures in each row. Have children circle the two pictures in each row that show different kinds of weather.

Pam

Hill Top School

1. Ted has a beautiful cat.

2. Kim likes to paint.

3. Turn left on Red Street.

4. It is often hot in June.

Proper Nouns
Explain that a proper noun tells the name of a person, place, or thing and that all proper nouns begin with a capital letter. Point to the examples at the top of the page. Tell children that *Pam* names a girl and *Hill Top School* tells the name of a school. Then read the sentences and point out the pictures with children. Tell them to circle the proper noun in each sentence.

1. kim and ed are with mom.

2. rick's cat jack can nap.

3. My birthday is in march.

March

Sun	Mon	Tue	Wed	Thu	Fri	Sat
			1	2	3	4
5	6	7	8	9	10	11
12	13	14	15	16	17	18
19	20	21	22	23	24	25
26	27	28	29	30	31	

4. Are we going to the zoo on saturday?

5. We go to wilson hill school.

Grammar: Proper Nouns
Remind children that a proper noun names a person, place, or thing. Then read each sentence and point to and name the pictures. Tell children to circle the words that should begin with a capital letter because they are proper nouns. Tell children to refer back to a piece of writing that they did during the week and make sure they used proper nouns correctly.

1. Did rick pack the bag

_____

- -

_____

2. she was Not sad.

_____

- -

_____

3. Can i go to the park

_____

- -

_____

4. He did not go

_____

- -

_____

Edit/Proofread

Tell children to listen as you read aloud the sentences. Have them rewrite each sentence so it shows correct capitalization and punctuation. Use gestures to clarify meaning. Then tell children to refer back to a piece of writing they did during the week and check that they used correct capitalization and end punctuation. Encourage children to use spelling patterns to help them write and to check that they spelled high-frequency words correctly.

Dad is back.

She can sip and nap.

Connect to Community
Encourage children to read the story to a family member or a friend.

Dad Is Back

She was sad.

Review High-Frequency Words
Have children set a purpose for reading, such as finding out what Dad does to help his sick little bear. Explain that words in a sentence are separated by spaces. Point to the space between the words *she* and *was* on page 1. Then ask children to point to the space between the words *she* and *was* on page 1. Then ask children to point to the letter *w* in the word *was*. Have children tell what the *w* represents and what *was* represents.

She was sick.

Dad sat on the bed.

She was hot.

Name _____

1.

_____

2.

_____

3.

_____

4.

Phonological Awareness: Identify Alliteration
Remind children that sometimes words in a sentence begin with the same sound. Say: *Billy bats a ball.*
Elicit from children that the words begin with the /b/ sound. Then say: *Billy is on a team* and point out that
the words do not begin with the same sound. Tell children you will say sentences aloud. Tell them to listen
to each sentence and draw a picture that describes the sentence that has alliteration in each set. 1. *Ron
races really fast. Ron can go on the bus.* 2. *Mack is funny. Mack may meet us at the market.* 3. *Lynn likes to
get lots of letters. Lynn has a cute dog.* 4. *Ed likes bananas. Ed and Ellen like eggs.*

1.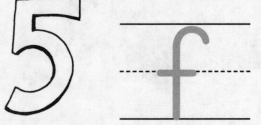

2.

3.

4.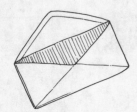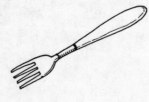

Phonics Review: /h/h, /e/e, /f/f
Point to and say the names of the pictures on the page. Have children write the letter that stands for the beginning sound in each picture's name next to the picture. Tell children to look at the pictures in each row from left to right. Then tell them to work their way from the top of the page to the bottom.

Name _____

1.

_____

- - - - - r - - - - - - -

- - - - - - - - - - - - - -

2.

_____

- - - - - - - - - - - - - -

- - - - - - - - - - - - - -

3.

_____

- - - - - - - - - - - - - -

- - - - - - - - - - - - - -

4.

_____

- - - - - - - - - - - - - -

- - - - - - - - - - - - - -

Phonics Review: /r/r, /b/b, /l/l
Point to and say the names of the pictures on the page. Have children write the letter that stands for the beginning sound in each picture's name next to the picture. Tell children to look at the pictures in each row from left to right. Then tell them to work their way from the top of the page to the bottom.

Name _____

I.  ck  _____

2.  _____  _____

3.  _____ 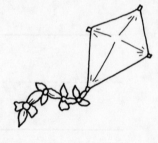 _____

4.  _____  _____

Phonics Review: */k/ k, /k/ ck*
Point to and say the names of the pictures on the page. Have children write the letter that stands for the beginning sound in some of the pictures' names and write the letters that stand for the ending sound in some of the pictures' names next to the picture. Tell children to look at the pictures in each row from left to right. Then tell them to work their way from the top of the page to the bottom.

Name _____

I.

 _____   _____

2.

 _____  _____

3.

 _____  _____

4.

 _____ 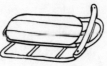 _____

Phonics: *bl, cl, fl, sl*
Point to and say the name of the first picture in row I. Say that it shows a block. Say: block *begins with the sounds /bl/.* Point out that the letters *b* and *l* together form the blend *bl.* Now point to and say the names of the rest of the pictures on the page. Have children write the letters *bl, cl, fl,* or *sl* for the beginning sounds next to each picture. Remind children to look at the pictures in each row from left to right and work their way from the top of the page to the bottom.

Name _____

black slid clam flat

1.  _____

- -

_____

2. B _____

- -

_____

3. _____

- -

_____

Phonics/Spelling
Decode Words: Say *flop* and point to your mouth position. Write the word and model how to decode it. Then have children decode the words at the top of the page. Spell Words: Point out to children that they can identify and spell words using a sound-spelling pattern, such as words ending with *-ock*. Model how to write the word that names the first picture, *rock*. Have children write the other words. Tell them that both words end with the spelling pattern *-ock*, as in *rock*. Then have them refer back to a piece of writing and use spelling patterns to correct spellings.

Name _____

1. little   she   my

2. with   was   are

3. he   is   little

4. my   she   was

Review High-Frequency Words
Have children follow these directions:

1 Circle the word *she*.   2 Circle the word *was*.
3 Circle the word *is*.   4 Circle the word *my*.
Say the words *my, was, she, he,* and *little* for children to spell.

Name _____

1.

2.

3.

Category Words: Question Words

Explain to children that the words *who, what, where,* and *when* are question words. The word *Who* asks about a person. The word *What* asks about something. The word *Where* asks about a place. The word *When* asks about a time. Point to and name the pictures in each row. Then have children follow the directions at the bottom of the page.

1. Circle the picture that shows who a story might be about.
2. Circle the picture that shows what a story might be about.
3. Circle a picture that shows where a story might take place.

Name _____

1.

2.

3.

Category Words Review
1. Circle the pictures in this row that show foods.
2. Circle the pictures in this row that show seasons or seasonal places.
3. Circle the pictures in this row that show kinds of weather.

Name _____

1. The cats hid in the _____
   _____ .

   bush   bushes

2. The _____
   _____ are on the shelf.

   book   books

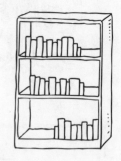

3. The _____
   _____ are in the sink.

   dish   dishes

Plural Nouns
Explain to children that a plural noun tells about more than one thing. Tell children that *bats* names more than one bat and *lunches* names more than one lunch. Then read the sentences and point out the pictures with children. Tell them to write the plural noun to complete each sentence. Then tell children to refer back to a piece of writing that they did during the week and check it for correct use of plural nouns. Encourage children to also use spelling patterns to help them write and to check that they spelled high-frequency words correctly.

_____

- - - - - - - - - - - - - - - - - - - -

1. Are the _____ on the bed?

sock   socks

_____

- - - - - - - - - - - - - - - - - - - -

2. The _____ nap in a den.

fox   foxes

_____

- - - - - - - - - - - - - - - - - - - -

3. The _____ are red.

dress   dresses

Plural Nouns
Remind children that a plural noun tells about more than one thing. Then read the sentences and point out the pictures with children. Tell them to write the plural noun to complete each sentence. Tell children to refer back to a piece of writing that they did over the week and check it for correct use of plural nouns.

1. "i like it," said Ned

_____

2. Can i go with you

_____

3. we can go to see Mack

_____

4. i can stop it.

_____

Edit/Proofread
Tell children to listen as you read aloud the sentences. Have them rewrite each sentence so it shows correct capitalization and punctuation. Use gestures to clarify meaning. Then tell children to refer back to a piece of writing they did during the week and check that they used correct capitalization and end punctuation. Encourage children to use spelling patterns to help them write and to check to see if they spelled high-frequency words correctly.

Tip, Tap

Tip, tap on my deck.

Review High-Frequency Words
Have children set a purpose for reading, such as finding out what the children do. Explain that words in a sentence are separated by spaces. Point to the space between the words *tip* and *tap* on page 1. Then ask children to point to the space between the words *my* and *deck* on page 1. Then ask children to point to the letter *m* in the word *my* on page 1. Elicit from children that the *m* is a letter and *my* is a word.

1

He is with my little cat!

Connect to Community
Encourage children to read the story to a family member or a friend.

We sit with my little cat.

We are in.
She was mad!

Draw

1.	2.
3.	4.

Phonological Awareness: Onset and Rime Blending
Say the word *run*. Then say /r//un/, *run*. Have children repeat. Explain that you first said the beginning sound in the word *run* and then you said the remaining sounds. Say that you blended the sounds together to say *run*. Tell children that you will say the beginning and ending sounds in some words. Have them blend the sounds together to say the word. Then tell children to draw a picture of the word in each box.
1. /s//un/, *sun*; 2. /n//ut/, *nut*; 3. /d//uk/, *duck*; 4. /p//up/, *pup*.

Phonemic Awareness: /u/

Point to and say the name of the picture of the umbrella. Tell children that the word *umbrella* begins with the /u/ sound. Have children repeat, *umbrella*, /u/. Now point to and say the names of the rest of the pictures on the page. Tell children to circle the pictures that have names that begin with the /u/ sound as in *umbrella*. Tell children to look at the pictures in each row from left to right and work their way down the page from top to bottom.

1.

2.

3.

4.

Phonemic Awareness: Phoneme Deletion

Say *bus.* Then take away the *b.* Say the new word that is formed: *us.* Point out that the word *us* was formed after you took away the first sound in the word. Name the picture in each row. Tell children to draw a picture in each row. Say that each picture should show what is formed after you take away the first sound in the word. Row 1: Take away the /c/ in *clap;* Row 2: Take away the /c/ in *cup;* Row 3: Take away the /f/ in *flip;* Row 4: Take away the /c/ in *clock.*

Uu

1.

2.

3.

4.

Phonics: /u/u

Point to and say the name of the picture of the undershirt. Tell children that the word *undershirt* begins with the /u/ sound. Explain that the letter *u* stands for the /u/ sound. Now point to and say the names of the rest of the pictures on the page. Have children write the letter *u* next to the picture if its name begins with the /u/ sound as in *undershirt*. Tell children to look at the pictures in each row from left to right. Then tell them to work their way from the top of the page to the bottom.

fun hum stuck club

1.  _____

2.  _____

3.  _____

4.  _____

Phonics/Spelling
Decode Words: Say *bud* and point to your mouth position. Write the word and model how to decode it. Then have children decode the words at the top of the page. Spell Words: Have children write the name of each picture on the lines.

1. **fun**   **flop**   **bun**

2. **duck**   **tuck**   **stack**

3. **mud**   **bud**   **man**

4. **nut**   **mud**   **but**

5. **run**   **rib**   **ran**

Phonics: Minimal Contrasts
Tell children that when you change one letter in a word, you make a new word. Write the words *hut* and *cut*. Explain that by changing the *h* in *hut* to a *c*, you make the word *cut*. Have children read the first word in each row. Tell them to draw a line under the new word that is formed when one letter in the word is changed.

I.

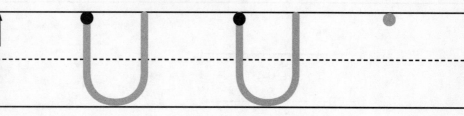

2.

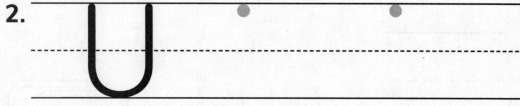

3.

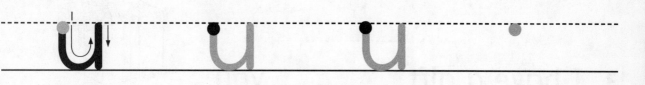

4.

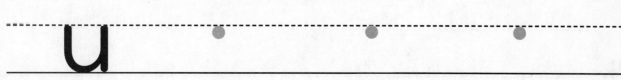

Handwriting: *Uu*
Model for children how to form the uppercase letter *U*. Say: *Straight down, curve around, straight up.* Then model how to form the lowercase letter *u*. Say: *Straight down, curve around, and up straight down.* Have children use their finger to trace the model for the letter. Then have them write the uppercase and lowercase forms of the letter *Uu*.

for	have	with

_____

1. I can go _____ you to the store.

2. Do you _____ the little clip?

3. I have a gift _____ you.

4. _____ .

High-Frequency Words: *for, have, with*
Model the Read/Spell/Write routine using the word *for*. Have children repeat the routine with *have*. Remind children that the other word at the top of the page is *with* and have them use the routine for the word. Then have children write one of the words to complete each sentence. Encourage children to then write their own sentence using one or more of the words. Have partners read the sentences to each other. Say the words *for, have,* and *with* for children to spell.

1.

2.

3.

Category Words: Animal Parts
Explain to children that animals have different characteristics. Some animals have wings; others have fur or hair; and others have tails. Tell children that some of the pictures on this page show animals that have certain characteristics in common. Point to and name the pictures in each row. Have children follow these directions: Circle the pictures of animals that have wings. Draw a line under the animals that have fur. Draw a box around the animals that have tails. Tell children to talk to a partner about the animals.

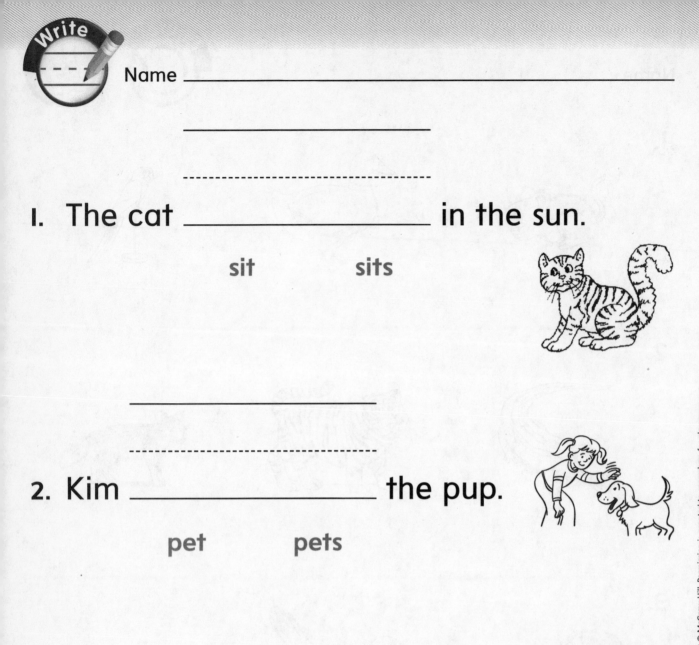

_____

----

1. The cat _____ in the sun.

     sit   sits

_____

----

2. Kim _____ the pup.

    pet   pets

_____

----

3. Sam _____ the socks.

    pack   packs

Grammar: Present-Tense Verbs
Explain to children that a present-tense verb tells what someone or something is doing. Tell them that the verb *eats* is a present-tense verb that tells what someone is doing now in the sentence *Mom eats her dinner*. Point out that the letter *s* is added to a verb if the verb is telling about one person or thing. Explain that when the verb is telling about more than one person or thing, there is no *s* at the end of the verb. Then read each example and the two answer choices. Point to and name the pictures. Tell children to write the verb that best completes each sentence on the lines.

Name _____

_____

----

1. The pup _____ with Ben.

plays   play

_____

----

2. Deb _____ to the hut.

hop   hops

_____

----

3. Nan _____ the cat.

pet   pets

Grammar: Present-Tense Verbs
Remind children that a present-tense verb tells what someone or something is doing now. Then read each example and the two answer choices. Point to and name the pictures. Tell children to write the verb that best completes each sentence. Then tell children to refer back to a piece of writing that they did during the week and check it for correct use of present-tense verbs.

1. ben likes The cub.

_____

_____

2. pam and tim can run.

_____

_____

3. Can i tuck my pet in bed

_____

_____

4. matt can see the duck

_____

_____

Edit/Proofread
Tell children to listen as you read aloud the sentences. Have them rewrite each sentence so it shows correct capitalization and punctuation. Use gestures to clarify meaning. Then tell children to refer back to a piece of writing they did during the week and check that they used correct capitalization and end punctuation. Encourage them to also make sure they used plural verbs correctly.

The pup is for you.

You have a pet!

Connect to Community
Encourage children to read the story to a family member or a friend.

4

Grade K · Unit 7 · Week 1

For You

You have a little duck.

It can hop for Mom!

Review High-Frequency Words
Have children set a purpose for reading, such as finding out what pet the little boy will get. Explain that words in a sentence are separated by spaces. Point to the space between the words *You* and *have* on page 1. Then ask children to point to the space between the words *for* and *you* on page 4. Model where to read when you get to the end of the first line. Have children read and point to where they read when they get to the end of a line on each page.

1

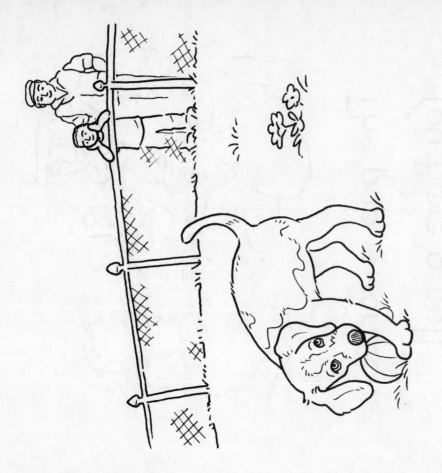

You have a little pup!

It can have fun.

You have a little pig.

It can rub the mud.

Name _____

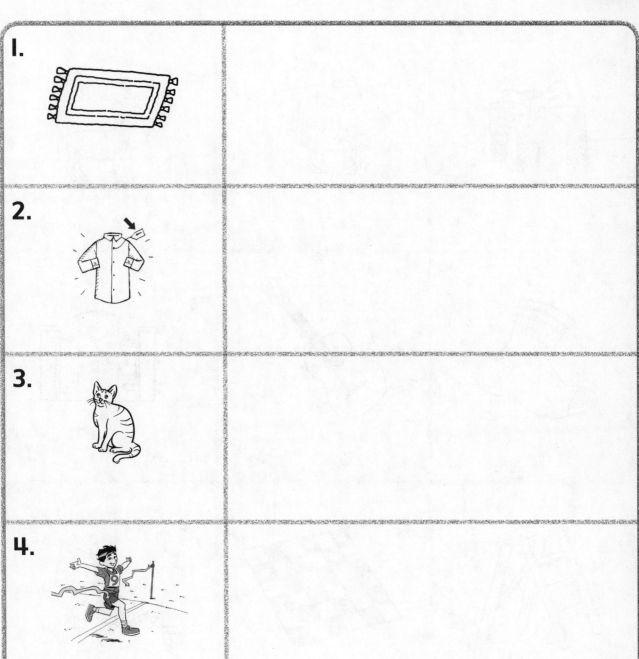

1.

2.

3.

4.

Phonological Awareness: Identify and Produce Rhyme

Remind children that words that rhyme have the same ending sounds. Say the words *get* and *bet*. Ask children if these words rhyme. Explain that these words rhyme because they end with the same sounds, /et/. Then ask them to name another word that rhymes with *get* and *bet*. Elicit that the words *let, met, net, set,* and *wet* also rhyme with these words. Now point to and say the name of the picture in each row. Then have children name the picture in each row and draw a picture of something that rhymes with that picture name in the empty space.

Phonemic Awareness: /g/

Point to and say the name of the picture of the gift. Tell children that the word *gift* begins with the /g/ sound. Have children repeat, *gift*, /g/. Now point to and say the names of the rest of the pictures on the page. Tell children to circle the pictures that have names that begin with the /g/ sound as in *gift*. Tell children to look at the pictures in each row from left to right and work their way down the page from top to bottom.

Name _____

Phonemic Awareness: /w/

Point to and say the name of the picture of the watermelon. Tell children that the word *watermelon* begins with the /w/ sound. Have children repeat, *watermelon*, /w/. Now point to and say the names of the rest of the pictures on the page. Tell children to circle the pictures that have names that begin with the /w/ sound as in *watermelon*. Tell children to look at the pictures in each row from left to right and work their way down the page from top to bottom.

Grade K • Unit 7 • Week 2   303

Name _____

I.

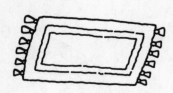  

2.

3.

4.

Phonemic Awareness: Phoneme Substitution

Say *get*. Then change the beginning letter *g* to an *l*. Say the new word that is formed: *let*. Point out that the word *let* was formed after you changed the first sound in the word to another sound. Repeat with the word *bug* and change the *u* to an *a* to form the word *bag*. Name the pictures in each row. Tell children to circle the picture in each row that is formed after you say the following: Row I: Substitute /b/ for /r/ in *rug* to form *bug*; Row 2: Substitute /a/ for /i/ in *wig* to form *wag*; Row 3: Substitute /m/ for /h/ in *hug* to form *mug*; Row 4: Substitute /e/ for /o/ in *log* to form *leg*.

Gg

Name _____

1.  _____

g _ _ _ _ _ _ _ _ _ _

 _____
_ _ _ _ _ _ _ _ _ _

2.  _____
_ _ _ _ _ _ _ _ _ _

 _____
_ _ _ _ _ _ _ _ _ _

3.  _____
_ _ _ _ _ _ _ _ _ _

 _____
_ _ _ _ _ _ _ _ _ _

4.  _____
_ _ _ _ _ _ _ _ _ _

 _____
_ _ _ _ _ _ _ _ _ _

Phonics: /g/ g

Point to and say the name of the picture of the gate. Tell children that the word *gate* begins with the /g/ sound. Explain that the letter *g* stands for the /g/ sound. Now point to and say the name of the rest of the pictures on the page. Have children write the letter *g* next to the picture if its name begins with /g/ sound as in *gate*. Tell children to look at the pictures in each row from left to right. Then tell them to work their way from the top of the page to the bottom.

Name _____

Ww

1.

_____

- - - - - - - - - -

_____

_____

- - - - - - - - - -

_____

2.

_____

- - - - - - - - - -

_____

_____

- - - - - - - - - -

_____

3.

_____

- - - - - - - - - -

_____

_____

- - - - - - - - - -

_____

4.

_____

- - - - - - - - - -

_____

_____

- - - - - - - - - -

_____

Phonics: /w/ w

Point to and say the name of the picture of the watch. Tell children that the word *watch* begins with the /w/ sound. Explain that the letter *w* stands for the /w/ sound. Now point to and say the names of the rest of the pictures on the page. Have children write the letter *w* next to the picture if its name begins with the /w/ sound as in *watch*. Tell children to look at the pictures in each row from left to right. Then tell them to work their way from the top of the page to the bottom.

gas   wet   win   wit

1. _____

2.  _____

3. _____

4.  _____

Phonics/Spelling
Decode Words: Say *get* and point to your mouth position. Write the word and model how to decode it by saying each sound and then blending the sounds together to say *get*. Repeat with the word *wet*. Then have children decode the words at the top of the page. Spell Words: Have children write the word that names each picture.

1. Gus   get   bus

2. pig   big   pat

3. wet   web   win

4. wag   web   wig

5. bug   rug   Ben

Phonics: Minimal Contrasts

Tell children that when you change one letter in a word, you make a new word. Write the words *tug* and *tag*. Explain that by changing the *u* in *tug* to an *a,* you make the word *tag*. Have children read the first word in each row. Tell them to draw a line under the new word that is formed when one letter in the word is changed. Tell children to read from left to right.

Name _____

1.

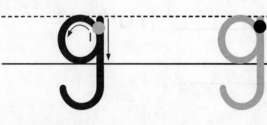

2.

3.

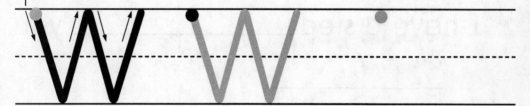

4.

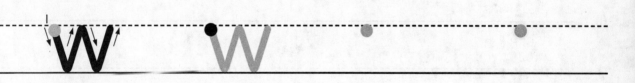

Handwriting: *Gg, Ww*
Model for children how to form the uppercase *G.* Say: *Circle back and around. Push up to the dotted line, and straight in.* Model how to form the lowercase *g:* Say: *Circle back, then around all the way. Straight down past the bottom line, and curl back.* Then model how to form the uppercase and lowercase *Ww.* Say: *Slant down, slant up, slant down, slant up.* Have children use their finger to trace the model for the letter. Then have them write the uppercase and lowercase forms of the letters *Gg* and *Ww.*

of	they	for

_____
- -

1. I had a piece _____ fruit.

_____
- -

2. I have a sled _____ you.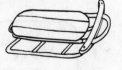

_____
- -

3. _____ have a bird.

_____
- -

4. _____

High-Frequency Words: *of, they, for*
Model the Read/Spell/Write routine using the word *of*. Have children repeat the routine with *they*. Remind children that the other word in the box is *for*. Tell children to repeat. Have children then write a word from the box on a line to complete each sentence. Then tell children to write a sentence using one or more of the words on the line. Have partners read the sentences to each other. Then say the words *of, they,* and *for* for children to spell.

Name _____

1.

2.

3.

Category Words: Pets

Explain to children that some animals make good pets while others do not. Say: *People can take care of pets, such as dogs, cats, and birds. People cannot have wild animals as pets.* Point to and name the pictures in each row. Have children circle the pictures in each row that show animals that could be pets. Encourage children to talk to each other about why the animals that they didn't circle would not make good pets. Have them also talk about ways to care for pets.

Grade K • Unit 7 • Week 2 **311**

Name _____

_____

----

1. Mom _____ the baby yesterday.

rocks   rocked

_____

----

2. Mack _____ a cap last week.

picks   picked

_____

----

3. I _____ my snacks for the picnic.

packs   packed

Grammar: Present and Past Tense Verbs
Explain to children that a verb can tell what is happening now as well as what happened already. Say: *jump* tells about something that someone is doing now as in *I jump high*. Then say: *The verb* jumped *tells what happened in the past as in* Yesterday the boy jumped. Then read each example and the two answer choices below. Point to and name the pictures. Tell children to write the verb that tells what happened in the past.

Name _____

Write

_____
----

1. Bob and Kim _____ a game.

played   plays

_____
----

2. Gus _____ the ball.

kick   kicked

_____
----

3. Pam _____ up.

jumped   jump

Grammar: Present-Tense and Past-Tense Verbs
Remind children that a verb can tell what happens in the present and what happened in the past. Then read each example and the two answer choices. Point to and name the pictures. Tell children to write the verb that tells what happened in the past on each line. Then tell children to refer to a piece of writing that they did during the week and make sure they used past-tense verbs correctly.

1. Did you have a lot of fun

_____

_____

2. "Yes, I did," rex said

_____

_____

3. ben said, "I w a n t to go."

_____

_____

4. i fed my cats

_____

_____

Edit/Proofread
Tell children to listen as you read aloud the sentences. Have them rewrite each sentence so it shows correct capitalization and punctuation. Use gestures to clarify meaning. Then tell children to refer back to a piece of writing they did during the week and check that they used correct capitalization and end punctuation.

They have a lot of fun!

They do not nap.

Connect to Community
Encourage children to read the story to a family member or a friend.

A Lot of Fun!

They have a lot of fun!

They like to tug.

Review High-Frequency Words
Have children set a purpose for reading, such as finding out how the animals have fun. Tell children that words are made up of letters and that there are spaces between words. Point to the first and last letters in the word *lot* on page 1 and the space between *a* and *lot*. Have children point to the first and last letters in *have* and the spaces before and after the word.

They have a log.
They like to nap a lot.

They have a pen.
They hop and hop!

1.	2.
3.	4.

Phonological Awareness: Onset and Rime Segmentation
Remind children that words are made up of beginning and ending sounds. Say the word *fix*. Tell children that the beginning sound is /f/. Then say that the ending sounds are /iiiks/, *fix*. Tell children to say the word, *fix*. Then say some words and encourage children to say the beginning and ending sounds in each word. Have children draw a picture in each box that shows the word. 1: *box, /b//oks/, box*; 2: *van, /v//an/, van*; 3: *six, /s//iks/, six*; 4: *vet, /v/ /et/, vet*.

Phonemic Awareness: /ks/

Point to and say the name of the picture of the box. Tell children that the word *box* ends with the /ks/ sound. Have children repeat, *box, /ks/*. Now point to and say the names of the rest of the pictures on the page. Tell children to circle the pictures that have names that end with the /ks/ sound as in *box*. Tell children to look at the pictures in each row from left to right and work their way down the page from top to bottom.

318 Grade K • Unit 7 • Week 3

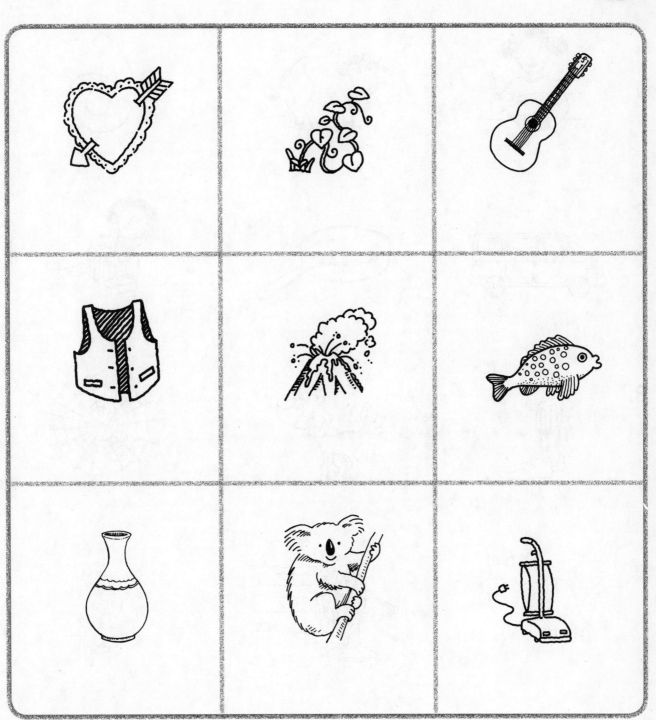

Phonemic Awareness: /v/

Point to and say the name of the picture of the valentine. Tell children that the word *valentine* begins with the /v/ sound. Have children repeat, *valentine*, /v/. Now point to and say the names of the rest of the pictures on the page. Tell children to circle the pictures that have names that begin with the /v/ sound as in *valentine*. Tell children to look at the pictures in each row from left to right and work their way down the page from top to bottom.

 Name _____

1.

2.

3.

4.

Phonemic Awareness: Phoneme Substitution

Say *lox*. Then change the beginning letter *l* to a *b*. Say the new word that is formed: *box*. Point out that the word *box* was formed after you changed the first sound in the word to another sound. Repeat with the word *six* and change the *x* to a *d* to form the name *Sid*. Name the pictures in each row. Tell children to circle the picture in each row that is formed after you say the following: Row 1: Substitute /s/ for /m/ in *mix* to form *six*; Row 2: Substitute /p/ for /v/ in *van* to form *pan*; Row 3: Substitute /g/ for /ks/ in *wax* to form *wag*; Row 4: Substitute /i/ for /o/ in *fox* to form *fix*.

Xx

Name _____

1.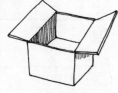

_____

_____

_____

_____

2.

_____

_____

3.

_____

_____

4.

_____

_____

_____

Phonics: /ks/ x

Point to and say the name of the picture of the box. Tell children that the word *box* ends with the /ks/ sound. Explain that the letter *x* stands for the /ks/ sound. Now point to and say the names of the rest of the pictures on the page. Have children write the letter *x* next to the picture if its name ends with the /ks/ sound as in *box*. Tell children to look at the pictures in each row from left to right. Then tell them to work their way from the top of the page to the bottom.

V v

I.  _____ 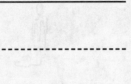 _____

- - - - - - - - - - - - - - - - - - -

_____

- - - - - - - - - - - - - - - - - - -

_____

2.  _____  _____

- - - - - - - - - - - - - - - - - - -

_____

- - - - - - - - - - - - - - - - - - -

_____

3.  _____  _____

- - - - - - - - - - - - - - - - - - -

_____

- - - - - - - - - - - - - - - - - - -

_____

4.  _____  _____

- - - - - - - - - - - - - - - - - - -

_____

- - - - - - - - - - - - - - - - - - -

_____

Phonics: /v/v
Point to and say the name of the picture of the violin. Tell children that the word *violin* begins with the /v/ sound. Explain that the letter *v* stands for the /v/ sound. Now point to and say the names of the rest of the pictures on the page. Have children write the letter *v* next to the picture if its name begins with the /v/ sound as in *violin*. Tell children to look at the pictures in each row from left to right. Then tell them to work their way from the top of the page to the bottom.

Name _____

lox   vat   ax   tax

1.

2.

3.

4.

Phonics/Spelling
Decode Words: Say *fix* and point to your mouth position. Write the word and model how to decode it by saying each sound in the word and then blending the sounds together to say *fix*. Repeat with the name *Vick*. Then have children decode the words at the top of the page. Spell Words: Have children write the word that names each picture. Then say the words *it, in, box, mix,* and *on* for children to spell.

Name _____

1. **fox**   **box**   **bus**

2. **van**   **vat**   **vet**

3. **six**   **sun**   **sax**

4. **mix**   **fix**   **fox**

5. **Vick**   **vat**   **Rick**

Phonics: Minimal Contrasts
Tell children that when you change one letter in a word, you make a new word. Write the words *vat* and *vet*. Explain that by changing the *a* in *vat* to an *e,* you make the word *vet.* Have children read the first word in each row. Tell them to draw a line under the new word that is formed when one letter in the word is changed.

Name _____

1.

2.

3.

4.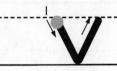

Handwriting: *Xx, Vv*
Model for children how to form the uppercase *X*. Say: *Slant down. Go back to the top. Slant down to cross.*
Then model how to form the lowercase letter *x*. Say: *Slant down. Slant in to cross.* Have children use their
finger to trace the model for the letter. Tell children how to form the uppercase and lowercase *Vv*. Say:
Slant down, slant up. Then have children write the uppercase and lowercase forms of *Xx* and *Vv*.

Grade K • Unit 7 • Week 3 **325**

said   want   have

_____

- - - - - - - - - - - - - - - - - - - -

1. Rick _____ he had fun at the party.

_____

- - - - - - - - - - - - - - - - - - - -

2. I _____ to go in the van.

_____

- - - - - - - - - - - - - - - - - - - -

3. They _____ two dogs.

_____

- -

4. _____

High-Frequency Words: *said, want, have*

Model the Read/Spell/Write routine using the word *said*. Have children repeat the routine with *want*. Remind children that the other word in the box is *have*. Tell children to repeat. Have children then write a word from the box on a line to complete each sentence. Tell children to write a sentence using one or more of the words on the line. Have partners read the sentences to each other. Then say the words *said, want,* and *have* for children to spell.

1.

2.

3.

Category Words: Animal Homes
Explain to children that animals live in different places. Say: *Some fish live in the ocean. Other fish live in rivers or lakes.* Say: *Monkeys live in trees. Bats live in dens.* Point to and name the pictures in each row. Have children circle the pictures in each row that show places where some animals live. Encourage children to talk to each other about why animals live in different places.

_____

----

1. Meg _____ a nap.

has   will have

_____

----

2. Vick _____ the bus.

fixes   will fix

_____

----

3. Rex _____ the deck.

will mop   mops

Grammar: Future Tense Verbs
Explain to children that a verb can tell what is happening now as in *The dog sleeps on the rug*. Other verbs tell about something that is going to happen. Say: *Mom will make dinner tells about something that Mom will be doing*. Then read each example and the two answer choices below. Point to and name the pictures. Tell children to write the verb that tells what will happen in the future.

_____

- -

1. Deb _____ Mom.

hugs   will hug

_____

- -

2. Rex and Dad _____ in the van.

will go   go

_____

- -

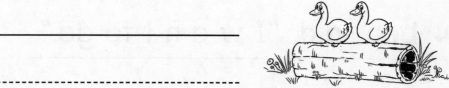

3. The ducks _____ on the log.

sit   will sit

Grammar: Future Tense Verbs
Remind children that a verb can tell what happens in the present. Say: *A verb can also tell what will happen in the future.* Then read each example and the two answer choices. Point to and name the pictures. Tell children to write the verb that tells what will happen in the future on each line. Then tell children to refer back to a piece of writing they did during the week and see if they used future tense verbs correctly.

1. Do You want to see it.

_____

_____

2. he said hewants to go on a jet.

_____

_____

3. i can Go.

_____

_____

4. ben said, "I w a n t to go."

_____

_____

Edit/Proofread
Tell children to listen as you read aloud the sentences. Have them rewrite each sentence so it shows correct capitalization and punctuation. Use gestures to clarify meaning. Then tell children to refer back to a piece of writing they did during the week and check that they used correct capitalization and end punctuation.

A Bed for Fox

"I see a bed," said Fox.

"I want to nap."

Review High-Frequency Words
Have children set a purpose for reading, such as finding out where the fox finds a bed. Explain that words in a sentence are separated by spaces. Point to the space between the words *want* and *to* on page 1. Then ask children to point to the letter *s* in the word *said* on page 1. Then tell children to point to the word *want* on page 4.

"I do fit," said Fox.

"I want to nap!"

Connect to Community
Encourage children to read the story to a family member or a friend.

Grade K · Unit 7 · Week 3

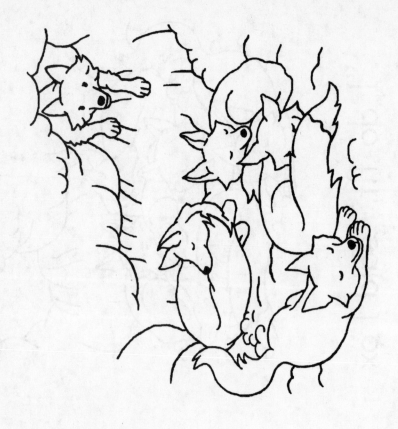

"I see a den!" said Fox.

"I want to fit."

"Mud!" said Fox.

"I do not like mud."

Name _____

Draw

1.	2.
3.	4.

Phonological Awareness: Syllable Addition

Explain to children that a syllable or word part can be added to another syllable to form a new word. Say the word *sun*. Point out that this is a one-syllable word. Then say the word *set*. Tell children that you are going to add the word *set* to the word *sun* to form the new word *sunset*. Repeat with the words *base* and *ball*. Then say the following words and ask children to say each one and then put them together to form a new word. Tell them to draw a picture in each box showing a picture of the word. Box 1: sun + rise = sunrise; Box 2: cup + cake = cupcake; Box 3: foot + ball = football; Box 4: skate + board = skateboard.

Grade K • Unit 8 • Week 1 **333**

Phonemic Awareness: /j/
Point to and say the name of the picture of the jet. Tell children that the word *jet* begins with the /j/ sound. Have children repeat, *jet*, /j/. Now point to and say the names of the rest of the pictures on the page. Tell children to circle the pictures that have names that begin with the /j/ sound as in *jet*. Tell children to look at the pictures in each row from left to right and work their way down the page from top to bottom.

334 Grade K • Unit 8 • Week 1

Name _____

Phonemic Awareness: /kw/

Point to and say the name of the picture of the quilt. Tell children that the word *quilt* begins with the /kw/ sound. Have children repeat, *quilt, /kw/*. Now point to and say the names of the rest of the pictures on the page. Tell children to circle the pictures that have names that begin with the /kw/ sound as in *quilt*. Tell children to look at the pictures in each row from left to right and work their way down the page from top to bottom.

Name _____

1.				
2.				
3.				
4.				

Phonemic Awareness: Phoneme Segmentation with /j/*j*, /kw/*qu*
Tell children to listen as you say the word *job*. Say each sound in the word *job*, /j//o//b/. Then blend the sounds together to say the word *job*. Explain that there are three sounds in the word. Name the picture in each row. Tell children to say each sound in the picture's name. Encourage them to count the number of sounds they hear and color in a box for each sound.

336 Grade K • Unit 8 • Week 1

Name _____

1.

_____

- - - - - - - - - - -

_____

_____

- - - - - - - - - - -

_____

2.

_____

- - - - - - - - - - -

_____

_____

- - - - - - - - - - -

_____

3.

_____

- - - - - - - - - - -

_____

_____

- - - - - - - - - - -

_____

4.

_____

- - - - - - - - - - -

_____

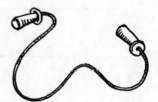

_____

- - - - - - - - - - -

_____

Phonics: /j/j

Point to and say the name of the picture of the jam. Tell children that the word *jam* begins with the /j/ sound. Explain that the letter *j* stands for the /j/ sound. Now point to and say the names of the rest of the pictures on the page. Have children write the letter *j* next to the picture if its name begins with /j/ sound as in *jam*. Tell children to look at the pictures in each row from left to right. Then tell them to work their way from the top of the page to the bottom.

Grade K • Unit 8 • Week 1   **337**

Name _____

1.  _____ 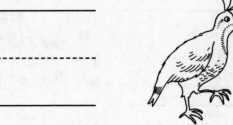 _____

2.  _____  _____

3. 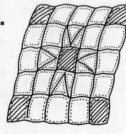 _____  _____

4.  _____ 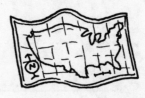 _____

Phonics: /kw/ *qu*
Point to and say the name of the picture of the queen. Tell children that the word *queen* begins with the /kw/ sound. Explain that the letters *qu* stand for the /kw/ sound. Now point to and say the names of the rest of the pictures on the page. Have children write the letters *qu* next to the picture if its name begins with the /kw/ sound as in *queen*. Tell children to look at the pictures in each row from left to right. Then tell them to work their way from the top of the page to the bottom.

job quit quick jog

1.

_____

- -

_____

2.

_____

- -

_____

3.

- -

_____

4.

- -

_____

Phonics/Spelling
Decode Words: Say *jot* and point to your mouth position. Write the word and model how to decode it.
Repeat with the word *quick*. Then have children decode the words at the top of the page. Spell Words:
Have children write the word that names each picture.

1. **quick**   **quit**   **quack**

2. **jot**   **job**   **jug**

3. **jam**   **Jim**   **pit**

4. **jug**   **jam**   **jog**

5. **jet**   **vet**   **Jan**

Phonics: Minimal Contrasts
Tell children that when you change one letter in a word, you make a new word. Write the words *jet* and *met*. Explain that by changing the *j* in *jet* to *m*, you make the word *met*. Have children read the first word in each row. Tell them to draw a line under the new word that is formed when one letter in the word is changed. Tell children to read from left to right and from top to bottom of the page.

Name _____

1.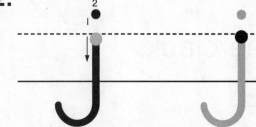

2.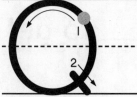

3.

4.

Handwriting: *Jj, Qq*
Model for children how to form the uppercase *J*. Say: *Straight down, curl back, then stop. Straight across the top line.* Model how to form the lowercase *j*. Say: *Straight down past the bottom line. Curl back, then stop, dot above.* Then model how to form the uppercase *Q*. Say: *Circle back, then around all the way. Slant down.* Model how to form the lowercase *q*. Say: *Circle back and around. Straight down. Curl forward.* Have children use their finger to trace the model for the letter. Then have them write the uppercase and the lowercase letters *Jj, Qq.*

> here   me   want

_____

- -

1. Jim is _____ by the clock.

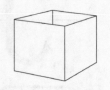

_____

- - - - - - - - - - - - - - - - - - - -

2. Do you want _____ to get a box?

_____

- - - - - - - - - - - - - - - - - - - -

3. They _____ to go on the jet.

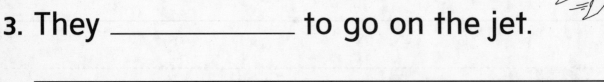

_____

- -

4. _____ .

High-Frequency Words: *here, me, want*
Model the Read/Spell/Write routine using the word *here*. Have children repeat the routine with *me*. Remind children that the other word in the box is *want*. Tell children to repeat. Have children then write a word from the box on a line to complete each sentence. Tell children to write a sentence using one or more of the words on the line. Tell children to point to the words *here* and *me* in the box at the top of the page. Have partners read the sentences to each other. Then say the words *here, me,* and *want* for children to spell.

1.

2.

3.

Category Words: Vehicles
Explain to children that there are different kinds of vehicles or transportation that can take someone from one place to another. Say: *A bus is a kind of vehicle. Some of you might take a bus to get to school.* Point to and name the pictures in each row. Have children circle the pictures in each row that show vehicles. Encourage children to talk to each other about the different vehicles and where they can go if they use them.

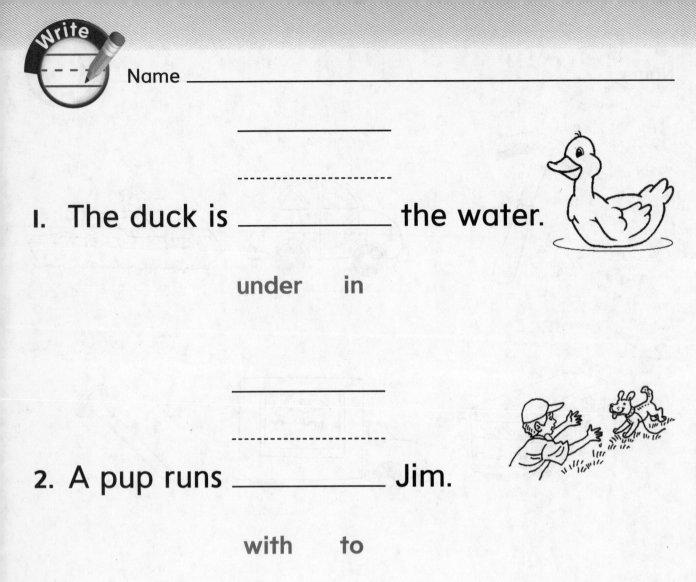

1. The duck is _____ the water.

under   in

2. A pup runs _____ Jim.

with   to

3. Jan can jog _____ the park.

on   in

Grammar: Sentences with Prepositions

Explain to children that a preposition is a word at the beginning of a group of words. The group of words tells more about who or what the sentence is about. Say: *The seal is in the water.* Explain that the word *in* is a preposition and the group of words "in the water" tells where the seal is. Point out that words such as *on, under, over* are all prepositions. Then read each example and the two answer choices below. Point to and name the pictures. Tell children to write the preposition that best completes the sentence.

Name _____

| to | in | on |

1. Bob will go _____ his job.

2. The frogs sit _____ the log.

3. The pigs are _____ the pen.

Grammar: Sentences with Prepositions
Remind children that a preposition is a word at the beginning of a group of words. This group of words tells more about who or what the sentence is about. *Listen to this sentence:* The book is on the table. *The word* on *is a preposition and the words* on the table *tell where the book is.* Read the sentences and point to and talk about the pictures. Tell children to write a preposition from the box on the lines to complete each sentence. Tell children to refer back to a piece of writing they did during the week and make sure they used prepositions correctly.

Name _____

1. jim has a cap for me

_____

- -

_____

2. The bug w a s in the web. it was stuck.

- -

_____

_____

- -

_____

- -

_____

Edit/Proofread
Tell children to listen as you read aloud the sentences. Have them rewrite each sentence so it shows correct capitalization and punctuation. Remind children that a sentence starts with a capital letter and ends with an end punctuation mark, such as a period. Use gestures to clarify meaning. Then tell children to refer back to a piece of writing they did during the week and check that they used correct capitalization and end punctuation. Tell them to also check to see if they used prepositions correctly.

Name _____

4

Connect to Community

Encourage children to read the story to a family member or a friend.

Can you see me?

Here I am!

Here I Am!

Review High-Frequency Words

Have children set a purpose for reading, such as finding out where the boy is. Explain that words are made up of letters. Point to the letter *h* in the word *Here* on page I. Then ask children to point to the letter *m* in the word *Here* on page I. Then ask children to point to the letter *m* in the word *me* on page 3. Ask children to say the word with the letter *m*.

Can you see me?

Here I am on the bus.

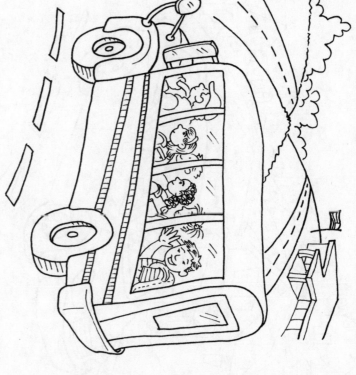

I

Can you see me?
Here I am in a jet.

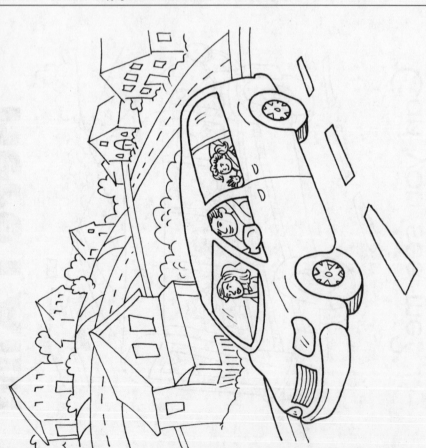

Can you see me?
Here I am in a van.

Name _____

1.

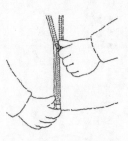

2.

3.

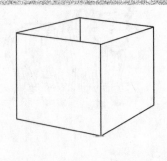

4.

Phonological Awareness: Identify and Produce Rhyme

Remind children that words that rhyme have the same ending sounds. Say the words *yet* and *get*. Ask children if these words rhyme. Then ask them to name another word that rhymes with *yet* and *get*. Elicit that the words *bet, debt, jet, let, met, net, set,* and *vet* also rhyme with these words. Now point to and say the names of the picture in each row. Have children then draw a picture of something that rhymes with that picture name in the empty space.

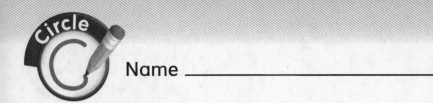

Phonemic Awareness: /y/

Point to and say the name of the picture of the yarn. Tell children that the word *yarn* begins with the /y/ sound. Have children repeat, *yarn*, /y/. Now point to and say the names of the rest of the pictures on the page. Tell children to circle the pictures that have names that begin with the /y/ sound as in *yarn*. Tell children to look at the pictures in each row from left to right and work their way down the page from top to bottom.

Name _____

Phonemic Awareness: /z/
Point to and say the name of the picture of the zoo. Tell children that the word *zoo* begins with the /z/ sound.
Have children repeat, *zoo*, /z/. Now point to and say the names of the rest of the pictures on the page. Tell
children to circle the pictures that have names that begin with the /z/ sound as in *zoo*. Tell children to look
at the pictures in each row from left to right and work their way down the page from top to bottom.

Name _____

1.

2.

  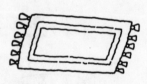

3.

4.

Phonemic Awareness: Phoneme Substitution

Say *yet*. Then change the beginning letter *y* to a *b*. Say the new word that is formed: *bet*. Point out that the word *bet* was formed after you changed the first sound in the word to another sound. Name the pictures in each row. Tell children to circle the picture in each row that is formed after you say the following: Row 1: Substitute /b/ for /y/ in *yak* to form *back*; Row 2: Substitute /r/ for /j/ in *jug* to form *rug*; Row 3: Substitute /n/ for /j/ in *jet* to form *net*; Row 4: Substitute /f/ for /v/ in *van* to form *fan*.

352 Grade K • Unit 8 • Week 2

Write

Name _____

1.  _____   Y    _____

2.  _____   _____

3.  _____    _____

4.  _____    _____

Phonics: /y/y
Point to and say the name of the picture of the yak. Tell children that the word *yak* begins with the /y/ sound. Explain that the letter *y* stands for the /y/ sound. Now point to and say the names of the rest of the pictures on the page. Have children write the letter *y* next to the picture if its name begins with the /y/ sound as in *yak*. Tell children to look at the pictures in each row from left to right. Then tell them to work their way from the top of the page to the bottom.

1.

 _____ z _____

2.

 _____ **0** _____

3.

 _____ **6** _____

4.

 _____ _____

Phonics: /z/z
Point to and say the name of the picture of the zoo. Tell children that the word *zoo* begins with the /z/ sound. Explain that the letter *z* stands for the /z/ sound. Now point to and say the names of the rest of the pictures on the page. Have children write the letter *z* next to the picture if its name begins with /z/ sound as in *zoo*. Tell children to look at the pictures in each row from left to right. Then tell them to work their way from the top of the page to the bottom.

354 Grade K • Unit 8 • Week 2

Name _____

yes   zip   yet   zag

1.

_____
- -
_____

2.

_____
- -
_____

3.

_____
- -
_____

4.

_____
- -
_____

Phonics/Spelling

Decode Words: Say *zip* and point to your mouth position. Write the word and model how to decode it. Repeat with the word *yak*. Then have children decode the words at the top of the page. Spell Words: Have children write the word that names each picture on the lines.

Grade K • Unit 8 • Week 2   **355**

1. **zag**   **zip**   **tag**

2. **yam**   **ham**   **him**

3. **yet**   **web**   **bet**

4. **zip**   **lip**   **zag**

5. **yum**   **yam**   **yuck**

Phonics: Minimal Contrasts
Tell children that when you change one letter in a word, you make a new word. Write the words *yet* and *set*. Explain that by changing the *y* in *yet* to an *s*, you make the word *set*. Have children read the first word in each row. Tell them to draw a line under the new word that is formed when one letter in the word is changed.

Name _____

1.

Y Y

2.

y y

3.

Z Z

4.

z z

Handwriting: *Yy, Zz*

Model for children how to form the uppercase letter *Y.* Say: *Slant down to the dotted line. Slant in to touch, then straight down.* Model how to form the lowercase *y.* Say: *Slant down. Slant in to cross, then down past the bottom line.* Then model how to form the uppercase *Z.* Say: *Straight across. Slant down to the bottom, straight across.* Model how to form the lowercase *z.* Say: *Straight across. Slant down to the bottom, straight across.* Have children use their finger to trace the model for the letter. Then have them write the uppercase and lowercase forms of the letters *Yy* and *Zz.*

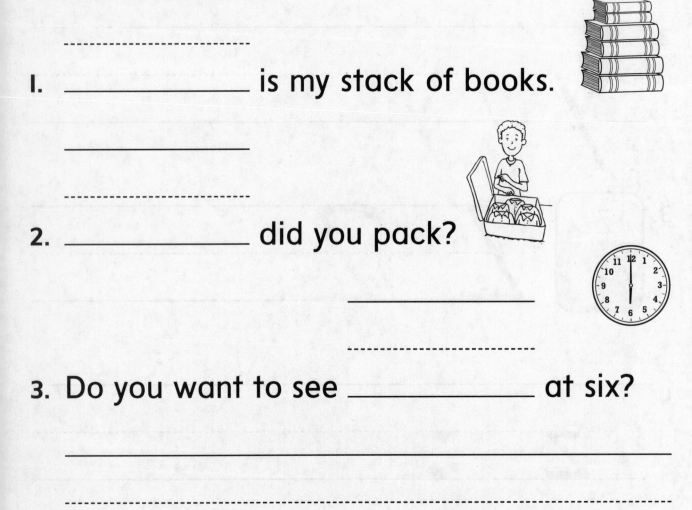

Name _____

| this   what   me |

_____

1. _____ is my stack of books.

_____

2. _____ did you pack?

_____

3. Do you want to see _____ at six?

_____

4. _____

High-Frequency Words: *this, what, me*
Model the Read/Spell/Write routine using the word *this*. Have children repeat the routine with *what*.
Remind children that the other word in the box is *me*. Tell children to repeat. Have children then write
a word from the box on a line to complete each sentence. Tell children to write a sentence using one or
more of the words on the last line. Have partners read the sentences to each other. Say the words *this*,
what, and *me* for children to spell.

Name _____

1.

2.

3.

Category Words: Location Words

Explain to children that location words are the names of places. Say: *The library is a place that you go to read and take books home.* Library *is a location word.* Say: *A school is a place that you go to learn.* School *is a location word.* Point to and name the pictures in each row. Have children circle the two pictures in each row that are places, or locations. Encourage children to use these place names, or location words, in sentences.

Name _____

_____

----

1. I sat _____ the chair.

on   off

_____

----

2. The yam is _____ the plate.

under   on

_____

----

3. Jack will go _____ cab.

on   by

Grammar: Sentences with Prepositions
Explain to children that a preposition is a word at the beginning of a group of words. This group of words tells more about who or what the sentence is about. Then read each example and the two answer choices below. Point to and name the pictures. Tell children to write the preposition that best completes each sentence.

under across behind

1. I am standing _____ her.

    off   behind

2. The duck can swim _____ the pond.

    under   across

3. The books are _____ the desk.

    under   on

Grammar: Sentences with Prepositions
Remind children that a preposition is a word at the beginning of a group of words. This group of words tells more about who or what the sentence is about. Read each example and the two answer choices below. Point to and talk about the pictures. Then tell children to write the preposition that best completes each sentence on the lines. Encourage children to refer back to a piece of writing that they did during the week and make sure they used prepositions correctly.

1. Can you get tim to go with you.

_____

_____

2. jim can see the big park?

_____

_____

3. What can i do for you.

_____

_____

4. Ted and rob had fun

_____

_____

Edit/Proofread

Tell children to listen as you read aloud the sentences. Have them rewrite each sentence so it shows correct capitalization and punctuation. Use gestures to clarify meaning. Then tell children to refer back to a piece of writing they did during the week and check that they used correct capitalization and end punctuation.

Name _____

Copyright © McGraw Hill

"We can do this!"

Connect to Community
Encourage children to read the story to a family member or a friend.

What Can You Do?

"This is for you."

"What can you do?"

Review High-Frequency Words
Have children set a purpose for reading, such as finding out what the girl does with the jump rope. Explain that words are made up of letters. Point to the letter *h* in the word *This* on page 1. Ask children what *h* is. Then ask children to find the words *They* and *What* on pages 2 and 3 of the story.

1

"What can we do?"

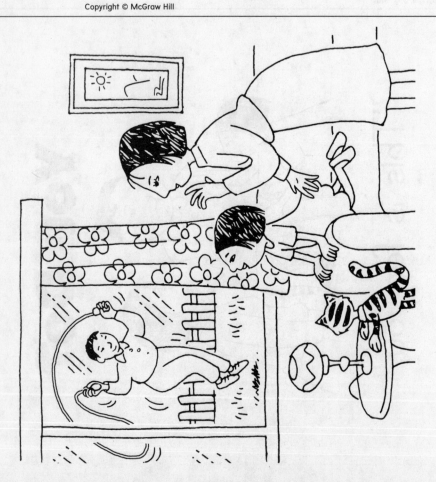

"I can do this," said Dad.

Name _____

1.	**2.**
3.	**4.**

Phonological Awareness: Syllable Deletion

Explain to children that a syllable or word part can be a word that can stand on its own. Say the word *football*. Point out that this word has two syllables or two parts, *foot* and *ball*. Then say the word *ball*. Tell children that you took away the first part of the word *football* and now you have the word *ball*. Repeat with the word *meatball*. Then have children follow these directions: Box 1: Take away the second syllable in the word *snowstorm*. Tell them to draw a picture in Box 1 showing a picture of the word that is left. Box 2: Take away the first syllable in *strawberry*; Box 3: Take away the first syllable in *pancake*; Box 4: Take away the first syllable in *carpet*.

Name _____

1.  _____  _____

_ _ _ _ _ g _ _ _ _ _ _ _ _ _ _ _ _ _ _ _

_____ _____

2.  _____ 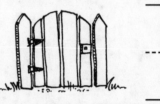 _____

_ _ _ _ _ _ _ _ _ _ _ _ _ _ _ _ _ _ _ _

_____ _____

3.  _____  _____

_ _ _ _ _ _ _ _ _ _ _ _ _ _ _ _ _ _ _ _

_____ _____

4.  _____  _____

_ _ _ _ _ _ _ _ _ _ _ _ _ _ _ _ _ _ _ _

_____ _____

Phonics Review: /u/u /g/g, /w/w
Point to and say the names of the pictures on the page. Have children write the letter that stands for the beginning sound in each picture's name next to the picture. Tell children to look at the pictures in each row from left to right. Then tell them to work their way from the top of the page to the bottom.

Name _____

1.

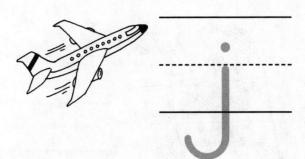

j

6

_____

2.

3.

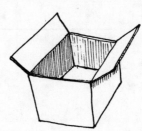

4.

Phonics Review: /ks/x, /v/v, /j/j
Point to and say the names of the pictures on the page. Have children write the letter that stands for the beginning sound in each the following picture names: jet, volcano, jar, violin, valentine. Then tell them to write the letter that stands for the ending sound in the following picture names: six, box, ax. Tell children to look at the pictures in each row from left to right. Then tell them to work their way from the top of the page to the bottom.

I.

_____
- -
z
_____

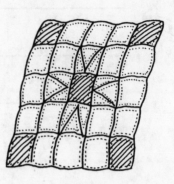

_____
- -
_____

2.

_____
- -
_____

_____
- -
_____

3.

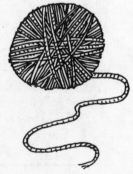

_____
- -
_____

_____
- -
_____

Phonics Review: /kw/ *qu,* /y/ *y,* /z/ *z*

Point to and say the names of the pictures on the page. Have children write the letter that stands for the beginning sound in each picture's name next to the picture. Tell children to look at the pictures in each row from left to right. Then tell them to work their way from the top of the page to the bottom.

Name _____

1.

br

2.

3.

4.

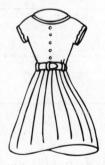

Phonics: Blends: *br, cr, dr, gr, tr*
Point to and say the name of the first picture in row 1, *brick*. Say: *Brick* begins with the sounds /b/ and /r/.
Point out that the letters *b* and *r* together form the blend *br*. Now point to and say the names of the rest of
the pictures on the page. Have children write the letters *br, cr, dr, gr,* or *tr* for the beginning sounds next
to each picture. Then write the words *drum* and *crib* on the board for children to decode.

Name _____

brag drop grin trot

1.  _____
   -
   _____

2. _____
   -
   _____

3. _____
   -
   _____

Phonics/Spelling
Decode Words: Say *trap* and point to your mouth position. Write the word and model how to decode it. Then have children decode the words at the top of the page. Spell Words: Model how to spell the word *kick* in the first example as you say the letter names. Then have children write the words for the next two pictures. Have children write the word. Remind children that some words end with the same sounds or have the same spelling pattern as in *can* and *tan*. Tell children to refer back to a piece of writing that they did during the week and make sure they used spelling patterns to help them write. Tell them to also make sure their high-frequency words are spelled correctly. Then say the words *drip, grip,* and *trip* for children to spell.

370 Grade K • Unit 8 • Week 3

1. they   have   me

2. here   said   of

3. for   this   what

4. want   here   said

Review High-Frequency Words
Have children follow these directions:

1. Circle the word *have*.   2. Circle the word *here*.
3. Circle the word *for*.   4. Circle the word *said*.

Say the words *have, here, for, said* for children to spell.

Name _____

1.

2.

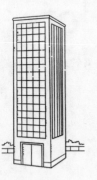  

3.

Category Words: Opposites
Explain to children that some words mean the opposite of each other. Say: I am turning the light on *and* I am turning the light off *mean the opposite of each other.* Explain that the words *on* and *off* are opposites. Point to and name the pictures in each row. Have children circle the pictures in each row that show opposites. Encourage children to talk to each other about their answers. Row 1: What other things do you do during the day and not during the night? Row 2: What other things are tall and small? Row 3: What other things are high and low?

Name _____

1.

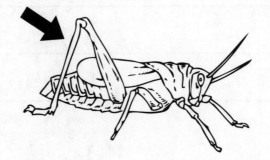

2.

3.

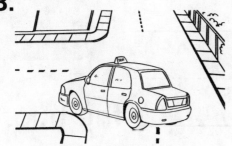

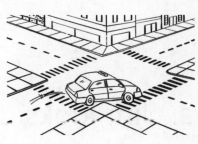

Category Words Review
1. Circle the pictures in this row that show an animal characteristic.
2. Circle the pictures in this row that show locations.
3. Circle the pictures in this row that show directions.

_____

----

1. Ned is _____ .

with the cat   in the cat

_____

----

2. The pen is _____ .

under the box   in the box

_____

----

3. Jim looks _____ the bug.

to   at

Grammar: Sentences with Prepositions
Remind children that a preposition is a word at the beginning of a group of words. This group of words
tells more about who or what the sentence is about. Then read each example and the two answer choices
below. Point to and talk about the pictures. Tell children to write the preposition that best completes the
sentence.

Name _____

_____

----

1. Dan runs _____.

on Rex   with Rex

_____

----

2. The sun is _____.

over the school   under the school

_____

----

3. Gus is _____ the bus.

off   on

Grammar: Sentences with Prepositions
Read each example and the two answer choices below. Point to and name the pictures. Tell children to circle the preposition or prepositional phrase that best completes each sentence. Then tell children to refer to a piece of writing that they did during the week and make sure they used prepositions correctly in their sentences.

1. is this what you want.

_____

_____

2. Can max go with us

_____

_____

3. dan said, "I have the b o x."

_____

_____

4. do you want to g o with me

_____

_____

Edit/Proofread
Tell children to listen as you read aloud the sentences. Have them rewrite each sentence so it shows correct capitalization and punctuation. Use gestures to clarify meaning. Then tell children to refer back to a piece of writing they did during the week and check that they used correct capitalization and end punctuation. Tell them to also check that they used prepositions and prepositional phrases correctly.

"I see me!" said Kit.

They have a lot of fun.

Connect to Community

Encourage children to read the story to a family member or a friend.

Jim and Kit

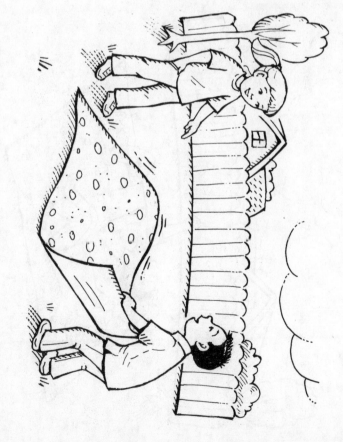

"Here it is!" said Jim.

"Do you want to sit?"

Review High-Frequency Words

Have children set a purpose for reading, such as finding out about Jim and Kit. Explain that words are made up of letters. Point to the letter *h* in the word *have* on page 4. Ask children what *h* is. Then ask children to point to the word *What* on page 2 and the word *This* on page 3.

"This is a little cup!"

"It is for you to sip!"

"What do you see?"

"I see a hen."

1.

2.

3.

4.

Phonological Awareness: Syllable Segmentation

Point to the pancake and say its name. Model clapping for each syllable in the word. Point out that there are two parts or syllables in *pancake*. Tell children that you will write the number 2 in the box because *pancake* has two parts or syllables. Point to and name the remaining pictures. Tell children to write a number on the line to show how many parts or syllables they hear.

Phonemic Awareness: /ā/

Point to and say the name of the picture of the cake. Tell children that the word *cake* has a long *a* sound.
Have children repeat, *cake, /ā/*. Now point to and say the names of the rest of the pictures on the page.
Tell children to circle the pictures that have names that have the /ā/ sound as in *cake*. Tell children to look
at the pictures in each row from left to right and work their way down the page from top to bottom.

Name _____

1.	2.
3.	4.

Phonemic Awareness: Phoneme Blending with /ā/
Tell children to listen to the sounds in the word *came*. Model blending the sounds to say the word *came*, /kāāāmmm/, *came*. Have children repeat. Tell children you will say the sounds in more words. Have them blend the sounds to say each word. Then have them draw a picture of the word: 1. /k/ā//k/ 2. /l//ā/k/; 3. /k//ā//p/; 4. /g//r//ā//p/.

1. 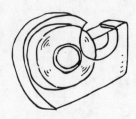 t a p e

2.  c k

3.  g t

4.  v s

Phonics: /ā/ a_e

Point to and say the name of the picture of the tape. Tell children that the word *tape* has the long *a* sound. Explain that the letters *a* and *e* stand for the /ā/ sound. Now point to and say the names of the rest of the pictures on the page. Have children write the letters *a* and *e* on the lines next to each picture. Remind children of the final *e* spelling rule. Say: *By adding the letter* e *to the end of some letters or words, it makes the vowel say its name. If I add an* e *to the end of the word* cap, *the word* cape *is formed.*

382 Grade K • Unit 9 • Week I

Write

ate maze quake blade

I.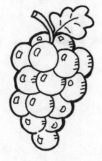

_____
- - - - - - - - - - - - - - -
_____

2.

_____
- - - - - - - - - - - - - - -
_____

3.

_____
- - - - - - - - - - - - - - -
_____

Phonics/Spelling
Decode Words: Say *bake* and point to your mouth position. Write the word and model how to decode it. Then have children decode the words at the top of the page. Spell Words: Have children write the name of each picture on the lines.

1. **bake**   bat   lake

2. **snake**   stake   state

3. **wade**   wave   was

4. **sale**   sand   tale

5. **rake**   rub   rave

Phonics: Minimal Contrasts
Tell children that when you change one letter in a word, you make a new word. Write the words *game* and *same*. Explain that by changing the *g* in *game* to an *s*, you make the word *same*. Have children read the first word in each row. Tell them to draw a line under the new word that is formed when one letter in the word is changed.

Name _____

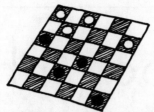

1. It is a game.

2. _____

3. It is a gate.

4. _____

Handwriting: *a_e*
Remind children about the proper formation of the letters *a* and *e*. Have children use their finger to trace the letters in the first sentence. Then have them write the sentence on the line. Repeat with the second sentence. Tell children to point to the space between each word.

Name _____

help	too	here

_____

- - - - - - - - - - - - - -

1. I can _____ you stand up.

_____

- - - - - - - - - - - - - -

2. Do you like grapes, _____?

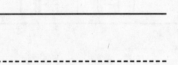

_____

- - - - - - - - - - - - - -

3. The trip starts _____.

_____

- -

4. _____

High-Frequency Words: *help, too, here*

Model the Read/Spell/Write routine using the word *help*. Have children repeat the routine with *too*. Remind children that the other word in the box is *here*. Tell children to repeat. Have children then write a word from the box on a line to complete each sentence. Tell children to write a sentence using one or more of the words on the line. Have partners read the sentences to each other. Then say aloud the words *help, too,* and *here* for children to spell.

Name _____

1.

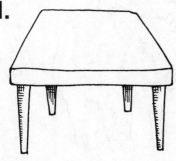  

2.

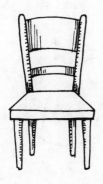  

3.

Category Words: Household Furniture

Explain to children that there are different kinds of furniture that can be in someone's home. Say: *A dresser, a bookcase, and a dining room table are types of household furniture.* Tell children that some of the pictures on this page show household furniture. Point to and name the pictures in each row. Have children circle the pictures that show household furniture.

Name _____

1. I see the _____ hog.

rug   big

2. I see a _____ bug.

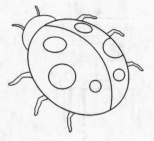

little   garden

3. Gabe gazes at the _____ flowers.

store   pretty

Grammar: Adjectives
Explain to children that an adjective is a word that describes a noun. Tell them that in the sentence *The smart boy reads, smart* is an adjective that tells about the boy. Then read each example and the two answer choices. Point to and name the pictures. Tell children to write the adjective that best completes each sentence on the lines. Tell partners to say sentences to each other that have adjectives.

Name _____

_____

----

1. Jane ate a _____ bun.

little   lake

_____

----

2. Jake had a _____ drink.

cold   glass

_____

----

3. I walk my _____ dog.

bone   big

Grammar: Adjectives
Remind children that an adjective is a word that describes a noun. Then read each example and the two answer choices. Point to and name the pictures. Tell children to write the adjective that best completes each sentence. Then tell children to refer back to a piece of writing that they did during the week and make sure they used adjectives correctly.

1. Abe and jane want to bake a cake

_____

- -

_____

2. Is the dog tame.can I pet it?

_____

- -

_____

- -

_____

Edit/Proofread
Tell children to listen as you read aloud the sentences. Have them rewrite each sentence so it shows correct capitalization and punctuation. Then tell children to refer back to a piece of writing they did during the week and check that they spelled words with spelling patterns, such as *-op, -et,* and *-am* correctly. Then tell them to check that they used spelling rules, such as adding an *e* to a part of a word to make the vowel say its name, as in *mak-make.* Encourage them to make sure they used adjectives correctly.

"I like to help!"

"I like to help, too!"

Connect to Community
Encourage children to read the story to a family member or a friend.

4

I Want to Help!

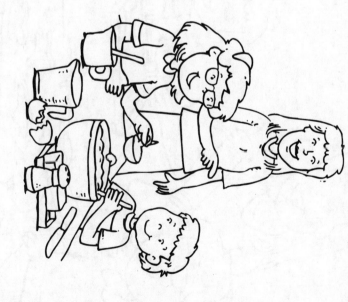

Pam can help mix.

Mack can mix, too.

Review High-Frequency Words
Have children set a purpose for reading, such as finding out how the girl and the boy help. Explain that we read from left to right. Model this concept of print. Then ask children to demonstrate it. Have children point to the words *help* and *too* and say them aloud.

1

Mom can help bake it.

"Can we help?"

Pam can help cut.

Mack can cut, too.

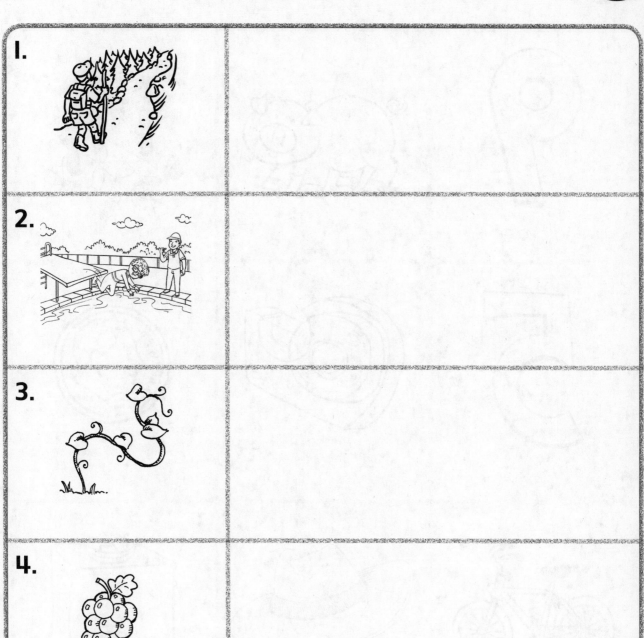

1.

2.

3.

4.

Phonological Awareness: Identify and Produce Rhyme

Remind children that words that rhyme have the same ending sounds. Say the words *fine* and *mine*. Ask children if these words rhyme. Then ask them to name another word that rhymes with *fine* and *mine*. Elicit that the words *line, sign,* and *vine* also rhyme with these words. Now point to and say the name of the picture in each row on the page. Have children then draw a picture of something that rhymes with that picture name in the empty space.

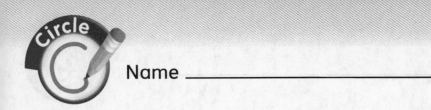

Phonemic Awareness: /ī/
Point to and say the name of the picture of the number nine. Tell children that the word *nine* has a long *i* sound. Have children repeat, *nine*, /n//ī//n/. Now point to and say the names of the rest of the pictures on the page. Tell children to circle the pictures that have names that have the /ī/ sound i as in *nine*. Tell children to look at the pictures in each row from left to right and work their way down the page from top to bottom.

394 Grade K • Unit 9 • Week 2

Name _____

1.

2.

 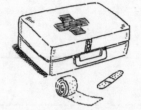 

3.

4.

Phonemic Awareness: Phoneme Deletion
Say *cold.* Then take away the beginning letter *c.* Point out that the word *old* was formed after you deleted the first sound in the word *cold.* Name the pictures in each row. Tell children to circle the picture in each row that is formed after you delete one sound: Row 1: Delete /t/ in *seat* to form *sea;* Row 2: Delete /e/ in *kite* to form *kit;* Row 3: Delete /f/ in *fox* to form *ox;* Row 4: Delete /t/ in *tape* to form *ape.*

Write

Name _____

5

i   y   i_e
igh   ie

1.

v i n e

2.

b t

3.

f v

4.

b k

Phonics: /ī/ i

Point to and say the name of the picture of the *vine*. Tell children that the word *vine* has the long *i* sound. Explain that the letters *i_e* stand for the /ī/ sound. Now point to and say the names of the rest of the pictures on the page. Have children write the letters *i_e* next to the picture if its name has the long *i* sound as in *vine*. Remind children that by adding the letter *e* to the end of some letters or words, it makes the vowel say its name. Say: *If I add an* e *to the end of* kit, *the word* kite *is formed.* Tell children that this spelling rule will help them spell some words with long *i* correctly.

396   Grade K • Unit 9 • Week 2

Name _____

mine quite slide drive

1.  _____

_____

_____

2.  _____

_____

_____

3.  _____

_____

_____

4.  _____

_____

_____

Phonics/Spelling
Decode Words: Say *mile* and point to your mouth position. Write the word and model how to decode it. Then have children decode the words at the top of the page. Spell Words: Have children write the word that names each picture on the lines.

1. time   Tom   tame

2. five   hive   flake

3. nine   name   fine

4. tile   Tim   time

5. line   lane   lot

Phonics: Minimal Contrasts
Tell children that when you change one letter in a word, you make a new word. Write the words *bike* and *bake*. Explain that by changing the *i* in *bike* to an *a*, you make the word *bake*. Have children read the first word in each row. Tell them to draw a line under the new word that is formed when one letter in the word is changed.

i y (i_e)
igh ie

Mike

1. I like Mike.

2.

5

3. He is five.

4.

Handwriting: *i_e*
Demonstrate to children the proper formation of the letters *i* and *e*. Have children use their finger to trace the letters in the first sentence. Then have them write the sentence on the line. Repeat with the second sentence. Tell children to point to the space between each word.

| has | play | too |

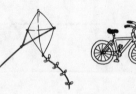

_____
- - - - - - - - - - - - - - - -

1. She _____ a bike and a kite.

_____
- - - - - - - - - - - - - - - -

2. Do you like to _____ a game?

_____
- - - - - - - - - - - - - - - -

3. I want to drive, _____ .

_____

- -

4. _____ .

High-Frequency Words: *has, play, too*
Model the Read/Spell/Write routine using the word *has*. Have children repeat with *play*. Remind children that the other word in the box is *too*. Tell children to repeat. Have children then write a word from the box on a line to complete each sentence. Tell children to write a sentence using one or more of the words on the line. Have partners read the sentences. Then say *has, play,* and *too* for children to spell. Tell children to point to *has, play,* and *too* as you say them. Then have children refer to a piece of writing they did this week and check that they spelled high-frequency words correctly.

1.

2.

3.

Category Words: Farm Animals
Explain to children that some kinds of animals live on a farm. Say: *A hen is an animal that lives on a farm.*
Tell children that some of the pictures on this page show farm animals. Point to and name the pictures in
each row. Have children circle the pictures that show farm animals.

Name _____

_____

1. _____ dog ran.

A   An

2. _____ ape is furry.

A   An

3. _____ logs are heavy.

The   A

Grammar: Adjectives

Explain to children that there are special adjectives, called articles, such as *a, an,* and *the*. Say that *a* is used with a noun that begins with a consonant. For example, in the sentence *A dog ran, a* is used with the noun *dog* because *dog* begins with a consonant. Say that *an* is used with a noun that begins with a vowel. In the sentence *An ape is furry, an* is used because the noun *ape* begins with a vowel. Then say that *the* can be used with nouns that name one or more things as in *The logs are heavy*. Then read each example and the two answer choices. Point to and name the pictures. Tell children to write the word that best completes each sentence on the lines.

Name _____

| an | the |

_____

1. _____ cave is dark.

2. _____ bike is fun to ride.

3. _____ ant is small.

4. Clive reads _____ funny book.

Grammar: Adjectives
Remind children that the words *a, an* and *the* are special adjectives called articles. Read the sentences and point to and name the pictures. Tell children to write the word from the box on the lines to complete each sentence. Then have children refer to another piece of writing that they did during the week and check it for correct use of the words *a, an,* and *the.*

1. Pam and jane play games

_____

- -

_____

2. Mike ate a bit of lime.He did not like it

_____

- -

_____

_____

- -

_____

- -

_____

Edit/Proofread

Tell children to listen as you read aloud the sentences. Have them rewrite each sentence so it shows correct capitalization and punctuation. Use gestures to clarify meaning. Then tell children to refer back to a piece of writing they did during the week and check that they used correct capitalization and end punctuation. Tell them to also check to see if they used articles correctly.

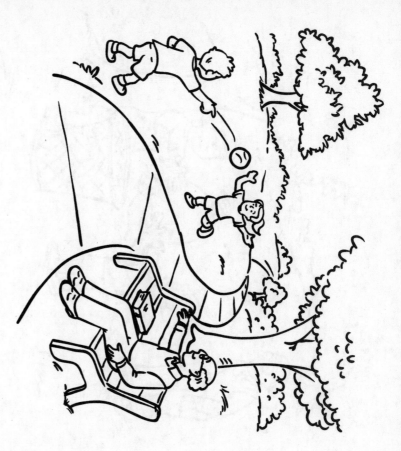

They can play here!

Connect to Community
Encourage children to read the story to a family member or a friend.

We Can Play!

We can not play here.

Review High-Frequency Words
Have children set a purpose for reading, such as finding out where the children can play. Explain that a word is made up of letters. Point to the letter *p* in the word *play* on page 1. Point out that this is a letter in the word *play*. Have children point to the letter *h* in the word *has* on page 3. Model return sweep and have children demonstrate it. Ask children to point to the words *has* and *play* in the story.

She has a big sack, too.

We put the sack in a bin.

We can help.

He has a big sack.

Name _____

1.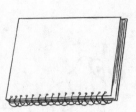

2.

3.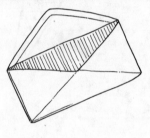

4.

Phonological Awareness: Segment and Blend Syllables

Say *homework*. Then say each syllable in the word *home* and *work*. Tell children that there are two syllables in this word. Clap as you model blending the syllables together to say *homework*. Tell children that you will write the number 2 on the board because *homework* has two syllables. Point to and name the pictures on the page. Tell children to say the syllables in each word and then blend them together to say the whole word. Have them write a number on the line to show how many parts or syllables they hear.

Phonemic Awareness: /ō/

Point to and say the name of the picture of the rope. Tell children that the word *rope* has a long *o* sound. Have children repeat, *rope*, /ō/. Now point to and say the names of the rest of the pictures on the page. Tell children to circle the pictures that have names that have the /ō/ sound as in *rope*. Tell children to look at the pictures in each row from left to right and work their way down the page from top to bottom.

Name _____

1.

2.

3.

4.

Phonemic Awareness: Phoneme Substitution
Say *note*. Then change the beginning letter *n* to a *v*. Say the new word that is formed: *vote*. Point out that the word *vote* was formed after you changed the first sound in the word to another sound. Name the pictures in each row. Tell children to circle the picture in each row that is formed after you say the following: Row 1: Substitute /k/ for /b/ in *bone* to form *cone*; Row 2: Substitute /s/ for /p/ in *rope* to form *rose*; Row 3: Substitute /l/ for /s/ in *hose* to form *hole*; Row 4: Substitute /p/ for /b/ in *robe* to form *rope*.

Name _____

o   oa   ow

o_e   _oe

1.

p   l

2.

c   n

3.

r   b

4.

h   s

Phonics: /ō/o_e

Point to and say the name of the picture of the pole. Tell children that the word *pole* has the long *o* sound. Explain that the letters *o_e* stand for the /ō/ sound. Now point to and say the names of the rest of the pictures on the page. Have children write the letters *o_e* next to the picture if its name has the long *o* sound as in *pole*. Remind children that by adding the letter *e* to the end of some letters or words, it makes the vowel say its name. Say: *If I add an* e *to the end of some words with a short vowel, such as* hop, *the word* hope *is formed.* Tell children that this spelling rule will help them spell some words with long *o* correctly.

note drove close spoke

1.

2.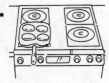

3.

4.

Phonics/Spelling

Decode Words: Say *rose* and point to your mouth position. Write the word and model how to decode it. Then have children decode the words at the top of the page. Spell Words: Have children write the word that names each picture. Explain that when you add the letter *e* at the end of the letters *n, o, t,* the vowel *o* becomes long and the word is *note*. The *e* at the end of the word makes the vowel say its name. Tell children that this rule will help them read and spell many words with long vowels.

1. **cone**   came   cove

2. **rose**   rope   rate

3. **drove**   dive   drive

4. **joke**   Jack   poke

5. **note**   vote   no

Phonics: Minimal Contrasts
Tell children that when you change one letter in a word, you make a new word. Write the words *so* and *go*. Explain that by changing the *s* in *so* to a *g*, you make the word *go*. Have children read the first word in each row. Tell them to draw a line under the new word that is formed when one letter in the word is changed.

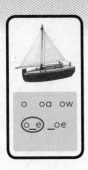

Name _____

o   oa   ow
o_e _oe

1. It is a rose.

2. _____

3.

I dig a hole.

4. _____

Handwriting *o_e*
Remind children about the proper formation of the letters *o* and *e*. Have children use their finger to trace all the letters in the first sentence. Then have them write the sentence on the line. Repeat with the second sentence. Tell chiidren to point to the space between each word.

Name _____

| where   look   play |

_____
- - - - - - - - - -

1. _____ do you take your sick pet?

_____
- - - - - - - - -

2. Do you like to _____ jump rope?

_____
- - - - - - - - -

3. _____ where you are going.

_____
- -

4. _____

High-Frequency Words: *where, look, play*
Model the Read/Spell/Write routine using the word *where*. Have children repeat the routine with *look*. Remind children that the other word in the box is *play*. Tell children to repeat. Have children write a word from the box on a line to complete each sentence. Tell children to then write a sentence using one or more of the words on the line. Have partners read the sentences to each other. Then say the words *where, look* and *play* aloud for children to spell. Have children point to each word on the page.

Name _____

1.

 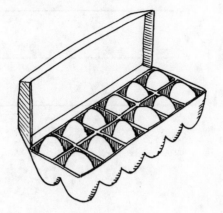 

2.

3.

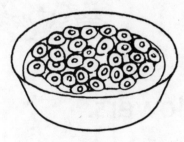  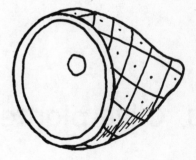

Category Words: Foods Made from Grain
Explain to children that some foods are made from grain or wheat, such as bread and popcorn. Point to and name the pictures in each row. Have children circle the pictures that show foods made from grain.

_____
----

1. We drove in a _____ van.

wide   nose

_____
----

2. Nate picked the _____ limes.

gave   ripe

_____
----

3. Clive planted _____ flowers.

garden   pretty

Grammar: Adjectives
Remind children that an adjective describes a noun. Tell them that the word *dinner* is an adjective in the
sentence *My dinner was delicious!* Then read each example and the two answer choices. Point to and
name the pictures. Tell children to write the adjective that best completes each sentence on the lines.

Name _____

_____

1. I like _____ music.

loud   soft

2. We like the _____ sun.

tame   warm

3. My _____ mom helped me.

wise   bake

Grammar: Adjectives
Remind children that an adjective is a word that describes a noun. Say the sentence: *The soft bunny is cute! The word* soft *in the sentence is an adjective, as it describes the noun* bunny. Then read each example and the two answer choices. Point to and name the pictures. Tell children to write the adjective that best completes each sentence on the line. Then tell children to refer back to a piece of writing that they did during the week and check that they used adjectives correctly.

1. jan gave the note to me.

_____

_____

2. Dad woke me up i did not want to get up.

_____

_____

_____

_____

_____

Edit/Proofread
Tell children to listen as you read aloud the sentences. Have them rewrite each sentence so it shows correct capitalization and punctuation. Use gestures to clarify meaning. Then tell children to refer back to a piece of writing they did during the week and check that they used correct capitalization and end punctuation. Tell children to also check to see if they used adjectives correctly.

418 Grade K • Unit 9 • Week 3

Look, it is big.

Where can it go?

Connect to Community
Encourage children to read the story to a family member or a friend.

Look at This!

Look, it is little.

What is it?

Review High-Frequency Words
Have children set a purpose for reading, such as finding out what the girl is looking at. Then ask children to point to the letter w in the word *Where* on page 4. Tell children to point to the high-frequency words *where* and *look* in the story. Have children set a purpose for reading, such as finding out what is little that turns into something big. Explain that words in a sentence are made up of letters. Point to the letter /i/ in the word *little* on page 1.

Look, it has a bud.
Can you see it?

It is in the sun.
It is hot.

Name _____

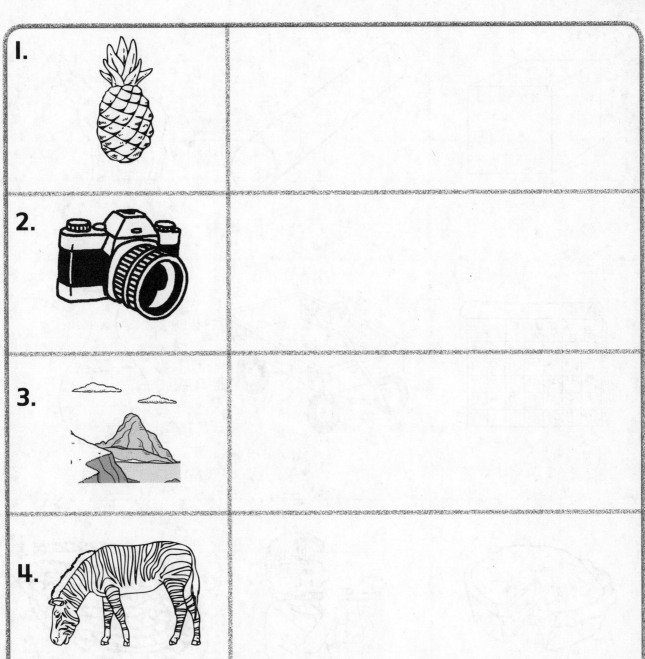

1.

2.

3.

4.

Phonological Awareness: Segmenting Syllables

Say *November*. Then say each syllable in the word. Model blending the syllables together to say *November*. Model clapping for each syllable in the word. Point out that there are three parts or syllables in *November*. Tell children that you will write the number 3 on the board because *November* has three syllables. Point to and name the pictures on the page. Tell children to say the syllables in each word and then blend them together to say the whole word. Have them write a number on the line to show how many parts or syllables they hear.

Phonemic Awareness: /ū/

Point to and say the name of the picture of the cube. Tell children that the word *cube* has a long *u* sound.
Have children repeat, *cube*, /ū/. Now point to and say the names of the rest of the pictures on the page.
Tell children to circle the pictures that have names that have the /ū/ sound as in *cube*. Tell children to
look at the pictures in each row from left to right and work their way down the page from top to bottom.

Name _____

1.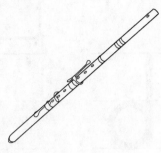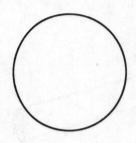

2.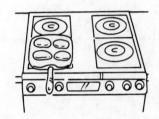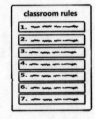

3.

4.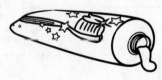

Phonemic Awareness: Phoneme Substitution
Say *cute*. Then change the beginning letter *c* to *fl*. Say the new word that is formed: *flute*. Point out that the word *flute* was formed after you changed the first sound in the word to two other sounds. Name the pictures in each row. Tell children to circle the picture in each row that is formed after you say the following: Row 1: Substitute /t/ for /b/ in *cube* to form *cute*; Row 2: Substitute /r/ for /m/ in *mules* to form *rules*; Row 3: Substitute /d/ for /f/ in *five* to form *dive*; Row 4: Substitute /n/ for /b/ in *tube* to form *tune*.

Grade K • Unit 10 • Week 1 **423**

Name _____

u u_e
_ew _ue

1.

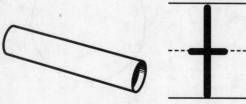

t u b e

2.

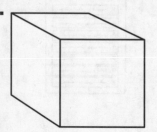

c   b

3.

d   k

4.

t   n

Phonics: /ū/ u

Point to and say the name of the picture of the tube. Tell children that the word *tube* has the *u* sound. Explain that the letters *u_e* stand for the /ū/ sound. Now point to and say the names of the rest of the pictures. Have children write the letters *u_e* next to the picture if its name begins with the long *u* sound as in *June*. Remind children that by adding the letter *e* to the end of some letters or words, it makes the vowel say its name. Say: *If I add an* e *to the end of the word* cut, *the word* cute *is formed.*

424   Grade K • Unit 10 • Week 1

Name _____

tube cute flute June

1.

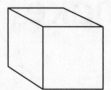

2.

3.

Phonics/Spelling

Decode Words: Say *tune* and point to your mouth position. Write the word and model how to decode it. Model saying each sound in the word and then blending the sounds together to say *tune*. Then have children decode the words at the top of the page. Spell Words: Have children write the word that names each picture on the lines.

Name _____

1. **cube**   **came**   **cute**

2. **mule**   **rule**   **make**

3. **tube**   **tune**   **dune**

4. **dune**   **drove**   **Dane**

5. **June**   **Jane**   **duke**

Phonics: Minimal Contrasts
Tell children that when you change one letter in a word, you make a new word. Write the words *rule* and *mule*. Explain that by changing the *r* in *rule* to an *m*, you make the word *mule*. Have children read the first word in each row. Tell them to draw a line under the new word that is formed when one letter in the word is changed.

u (u_e)
_ew _ue

Name _____

JUNE

S	M	T	W	T	F	S
		1	2	3	4	5
6	7	8	9	10	11	12
13	14	15	16	17	18	19
20	21	22	23	24	25	26
27	28	29	30			

1. It is June.

2.

3. Play a tune!

4.

Handwriting u_e
Remind children about the proper formation of the letters *u* and *e*. Have children use their finger to trace all the letters in the first sentence. Then have them write the sentence on the line. Repeat with the second sentence. Tell children to point to the space between each word.

Grade K • Unit 10 • Week 1 **427**

Name _____

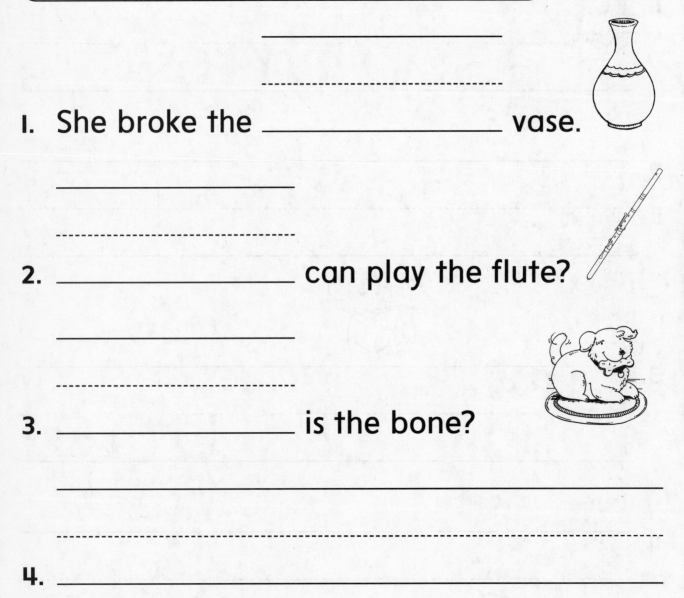

| good | who | where |

_____
- - - - - - - - - - - - - - - - - -

1. She broke the _____ vase.

_____
- - - - - - - - - - - - - - - - - -

2. _____ can play the flute?

_____
- - - - - - - - - - - - - - - - - -

3. _____ is the bone?

_____
- -

4. _____

High-Frequency Words: *good, who, where*
Model the Read/Spell/Write routine using the word *good*. Have children repeat the routine with *who*. Remind children that the other word in the box is *where*. Tell children to repeat. Have children then write a word from the box on a line to complete each sentence. Tell children to write a sentence using one or more of the words on the line. Have partners read the sentences to each other. Then say the words *good, who,* and *where* aloud for children to spell.

428 Grade K • Unit 10 • Week I

Name _____

1.

2.

3.

Category Words: Direction Words

Explain that some words name directions, such as *right* and *left*. Point to and name the pictures. Have children tell you the direction word in each sentence and then circle the picture:

Row 1: Circle the picture of the pig turning right on the path.

Row 2: Circle the picture of the duck turning left to the river.

Row 3: Circle the picture of the rabbit turning right to get to a big tree.

Have partners talk about the pictures, and words that name directions, and use the words in sentences.

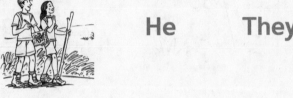

Write

Name _____

1. <u>Mom and Dad</u> like to hike. _____

He   They

2. <u>Meg</u> rode the bus. _____

We   She

3. <u>The rose</u> is red. _____

He   It

Grammar: Subjective Pronouns
Explain to children that a pronoun takes the place of something, someone, or more than one person. Write the following sentence on the board. *The sky is blue.* Under that sentence, write *It is blue.* Explain that *It* takes the place of *the sky.* Then read each example and the two answer choices. Point to and name the pictures. Tell children to circle the pronoun that can take the place of the underlined word(s).

1. <u>Kim and Ed</u> ate carrots. _____

We   They

2. <u>Mike</u> will ride the bike. _____

She   He

3. <u>Ed and I</u> made a cake. _____

We   They

Grammar: Subjective Pronouns
Remind children that a pronoun takes the place of something, someone, or more than one person. Then read each example and the two answer choices. Point to and name the pictures. Tell children to write the pronoun that best takes the place of the underlined words. Have children refer back to a piece of writing that they did during the week to make sure they used pronouns correctly.

1. who can go with us

_____

- -

_____

2. the name of my little dog is Max. He is a good dog?

_____

- -

_____

_____

- -

_____

_____

- -

_____

Edit/Proofread
Tell children to listen as you read aloud the sentences. Have them rewrite each sentence so it shows correct capitalization and punctuation. Use gestures to clarify meaning. Then tell children to refer back to a piece of writing they did during the week and check that they used correct capitalization and end punctuation.

Sam is good at this.

He can help mop.

Connect to Community
Encourage children to read the story to a family member or a friend.

4

Who Can Help?

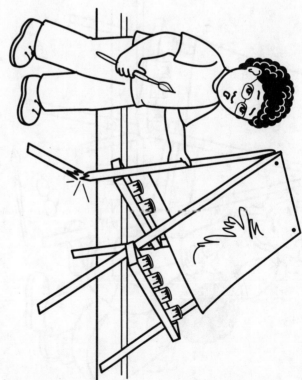

This is not good!

Who can I get to help?

Review High-Frequency Words
Have children set a purpose for reading, such as finding out how the girl helps. Explain that we read from left to right. Model this concept of print. Then ask children to demonstrate it. Model return sweep as well and then ask children to demonstrate it.

1

This is not good.

Who can help mop?

Deb can help me fix it.

She is good at this.

Name _____

1.	2.
3.	4.

Phonological Awareness: Syllable Substitution

Say *sunset*. Point out that this word has two syllables or parts. Tell children you are going to change the second part of the word *set* to *rise*. Say the new word that is formed: *sunrise*. Tell children you are going to change parts of words to other parts to form new words. Tell them to draw a picture of the new word. Say *panda*. Change the syllable *da* in *panda* to *cake*. Row 2: Change the syllable *storm* in *rainstorm* to *bow*; Row 3: Change the syllable *buc* in *bucket* to *bas*. Row 4: Change the syllable *black* in *blackboard* to *skate*.

Name _____

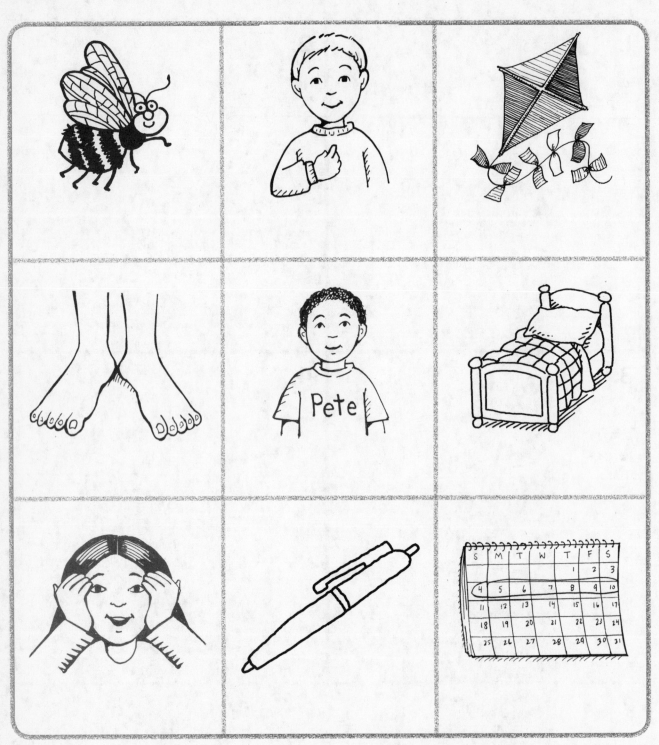

Phonemic Awareness: /ē/

Point to and say the name of the picture of the bee. Tell children that the word *bee* has a long *e* sound. Have children repeat, *bee*, /ē/. Now point to and say the names of the rest of the pictures on the page. Tell children to circle the pictures that have names that have the /ē/ sound as in *bee*. Tell children to look at the pictures in each row from left to right and work their way down the page from top to bottom.

436 Grade K • Unit 10 • Week 2

1.

2.

3.

4.

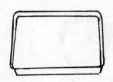

Phonemic Awareness: Phoneme Substitution
Say *me.* Then change the beginning letter *m* to a *w.* Say the new word that is formed: *we.* Point out that the word *we* was formed after you changed the first sound in the word to another sound. Name the pictures in each row. Tell children to circle the picture in each row that is formed after you say the following:
Row 1: Substitute /k/ for /b/ in *bee* to form *key;* Row 2: Substitute /p/ for /t/ in *sleet* to form *sleep;*
Row 3: Substitute /p/ for /b/ in *beak* to form *peek;* Row 4: Substitute /tr/ for /n/ in *knee* to form *tree.*

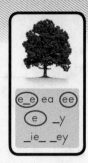

1.

— — —
m e

2.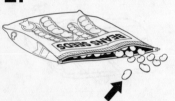

s — — d

3.

p — — k

4.

P — t

Phonics: /ē/ ee, e_e, e
Point to and say the name of the picture of the boy pointing to himself. Tell children that the word *me* has the ē sound. Explain that the letters *ee, e_e,* and *e* stand for the /ē/ sound. Now point to and say the names of the rest of the pictures on the page. Have children write the letters *e, ee,* or *e_e* next to the picture if its name has the long *e* sound as in *me*. Tell children to look at each row from left to right. Then tell them to work their way from the top of the page to the bottom.

Name _____

speed greet creek green

1. 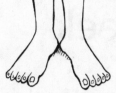 _____

2.  _____

3.  _____

4.  _____

Phonics/Spelling
Decode Words: Say *seed* and point to your mouth position. Write the word and model how to decode it. Model saying each sound in the word and then blending the sounds together to say *seed*. Then have children decode the words at the top of the page. Spell Words: Have children write the word that stands for each picture on the lines.

1. **bee**   **bus**   **see**

2. **keep**   **peep**   **peek**

3. **sleet**   **speed**   **sleep**

4. **seed**   **slope**   **seek**

5. **creek**   **creep**   **clam**

Phonics: Minimal Contrasts
Tell children that when you change one letter in a word, you make a new word. Write the words *reed* and *reef*. Explain that by changing the *d* in *reed* to an *f*, you make the word *reef*. Have children read the first word in each row. Tell them to draw a line under the new word that is formed when one letter in the word is changed.

Name _____

1. I see a bee.

2. _____

3. I see Eve.

4. _____

Handwriting *ee, e, e_e*
Remind children about the proper formation of the letter *e*. Have children use their finger to trace all the letters in the first sentence. Then have them write the sentence on the line. Repeat with the second sentence. Tell children to point to the space between each word.

| come | does | who |

_____

- - - - - - - - - - -

1. She can _____ and help.

_____

- - - - - - - - -

2. _____ sees the nest in the tree?

_____

- - - - - - - - -

3. _____ Zeke like to play music?

_____

- -

4. _____

High-Frequency Words: *come, does, who*
Model the Read/Spell/Write routine using the word *come*. Have children repeat the routine with *does*. Remind children that the other word in the box is *who*. Tell children to repeat. Have children then write a word from the box on a line to complete each sentence. Tell children to write a sentence using one or more of the words on the line. Have partners read the sentences to each other. Then say the words *come*, *does*, and *who* aloud for children to spell.

1.

2.

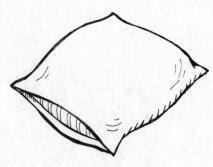  

3.

Category Words: Opposites
Explain to children that some words mean the opposite of each other. Say: *The words* hot *and* cold *are opposites.* Point to and name the pictures in each row. Have children circle the pictures that show opposites.

| them | her | him |

1. Kate gave the book to _____ .

2. Eve walks with _____ .

3. The bird belongs to _____ .

Grammar: Objective Pronouns
Remind children that a pronoun can take the place of something, someone, or more than one person.
Explain that one kind of pronoun, including *me, you, him, her, it, us,* and *them,* can come after a verb.
Read the sentence: *The teacher called him.* Say: *This kind of pronoun can also come after a preposition, such as in the sentence* The apples are for them. Read the pronouns at the top of the page. Then read the sentences and name the pictures. Tell children to choose a pronoun from the box and write it on the line to complete each sentence.

them	me	her

1. My sister gave the pen to _____ .

2. I am talking to _____ .

3. The man gave the flute to _____ .

Grammar: Objective Pronouns
Explain to children that a pronoun takes the place of something, someone, or more than one person. Read the sentences and point to and name the pictures. Tell children to choose a pronoun from the box and write it on a line to complete each sentence. Then tell children to refer back to a piece of writing they did during the week and make sure they used object pronouns correctly.

1. Can Zeke and i use the tape.

   _____

   -

   _____

2. We Need to tape the box?

   _____

   -

   _____

3. come and see what zeke and I made!

   _____

   -

   _____

Edit/Proofread
Tell children to listen as you read aloud the sentences. Have them rewrite each sentence so it shows correct capitalization and punctuation. Use gestures to clarify meaning. Then tell children to refer back to a piece of writing they did during the week and check that they used correct capitalization and end punctuation. Encourage children to use the Read/Spell/Write routine to make sure they spelled their high-frequency words correctly.

Name _____

It does fit in here!
Come and see!

Connect to Community
Encourage children to read the story to a family member or a friend.

4

Grade K · Unit 10 · Week 2

Come and See

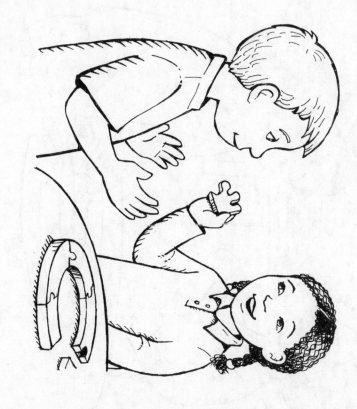

Can you help me?
Where does it go?

Review High-Frequency Words
Have children set a purpose for reading, such as finding out where the missing puzzle piece goes. Explain that a word is made up of letters. Point to the letter e in the word *does*. Point out that this is a letter in the word *does*. Have children point to the letter e in the word *come* on page 4.

1

Come and see this!

Does it go in here?

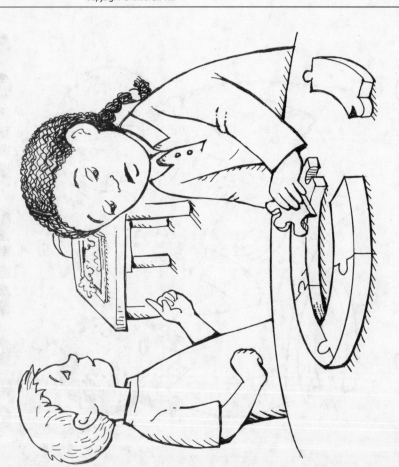

Does it fit here?

No, it does not fit.

Name _____

1.

2.

3.

4.

Phonological Awareness: Produce Alliteration
Remind children that some words in sentences can begin with the same sound. Have them name the sound that begins most words in the following sentence: *Tigers tiptoe to the tunnel.* Point to and say the picture name in each row. Then have them draw two things that begin with the same sound as the picture name in the space provided. Then challenge children to create an alliterative phrase or sentence.

Grade K • Unit 10 • Week 3   **449**

Name _____

I.  _____  _____

2. 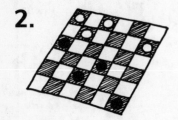 _____ 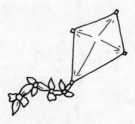 _____

3.  _____  _____

4.  _____ 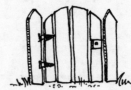 _____

Phonics Review: /ā/a_e; /ī/i_e
Point to and say the names of the pictures on the page. Have children write the letters that stand for the vowel sound in each picture's name next to the picture. Tell children to look at the pictures in each row from left to right. Then tell them to work their way from the top of the page to the bottom.

1.

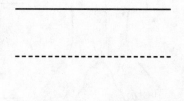

_____

- - - - - - - - - - - - -

_____

- - - - - - - - - - - - -

2.

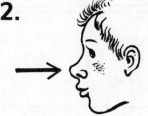

_____

- - - - - - - - - - - - -

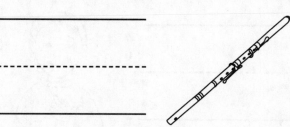

_____

- - - - - - - - - - - - -

3.

_____

- - - - - - - - - - - - -

_____

- - - - - - - - - - - - -

4.

_____

- - - - - - - - - - - - -

_____

- - - - - - - - - - - - -

Phonics Review: /ō/o_e; /ū/u_e
Point to and say the names of the pictures on the page. Have children write the letters that stand for the vowel sound in each picture's name next to the picture. Tell children to look at the pictures in each row from left to right. Then tell them to work their way from the top of the page to the bottom.

Name _____

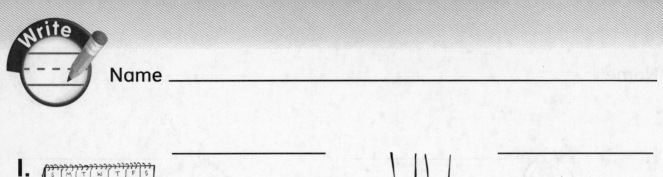

1.

2.

3.

4.

Phonics Review: /ē/; e_e, ee, ee
Point to and say the names of the pictures on the page. Have children write the letter or letters that stand for the vowel sound in each picture's name next to the picture. Tell children to look at the pictures in each row from left to right. Then tell them to work their way from the top of the page to the bottom.

452 Grade K • Unit 10 • Week 3

Name _____

I.

_____

- - - - - - - - - - - -

_____

2.

_____

- - - - - - - - - - - -

_____

3.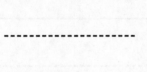

_____

- - - - - - - - - - - -

_____

4.

_____

- - - - - - - - - - - -

_____

Phonics: Final Blends: _st, nd, nk_
Point to and say the name of the first picture in row I. Say that it shows a nest. Say: Nest _ends with the sounds_ /st/. Point out that the letters _s_ and _t_ together form the blend _st_. Now point to and say the names of the rest of the pictures on the page. Have children write the letters _st, nd,_ or _nk_ for the ending sounds next to each picture. Remind children to look at the pictures in each row from left to right and work their way from the top of the page to the bottom.

most   bank   land   wink

1.

2.

3.

4.

Phonics/Spelling

Decode Words: Say *best* and point to your mouth position. Write *best* and model how to decode it. Repeat with *wink* and *sand*. Have children decode the words at the top of the page. Spell Words: Rows 1, 2: Identify the pictures on the page. Then have children write the word that names each picture. Tell them to use a spelling pattern to write the words, as the two words end with the same sounds. Rows 3, 4: Have children write the word that names each picture. Tell them to use a spelling pattern to write the words, as the two words end with the same sounds. Have children refer back to a piece of writing they did and use spelling patterns to check spelling.

Name _____

1.   too   play   who

2.   does   look   come

3.   who   does   where

4.   too   help   good

Review High-Frequency Words
Have children follow these directions:

1 Circle the word *play*.   2 Circle the word *does*.
3 Circle the word *where*.   4 Circle the word *good*.

Have children point to and say the words *help*, *does*, *come* and *who*.

1.

2.

3.

Category Words: Names of Baby Animals
Explain to children that the name of a baby animal can be different from the mother's name. Say: *A baby dog is called a puppy.* Point to and name the pictures in each row. Have children circle the pictures that show baby animals.

Name _____

1.

2.

3.

Category Words Review
1 Circle the pictures in this row that show directions.
2 Circle the pictures in this row that show opposites.
3 Circle the pictures in this row that show baby animals.

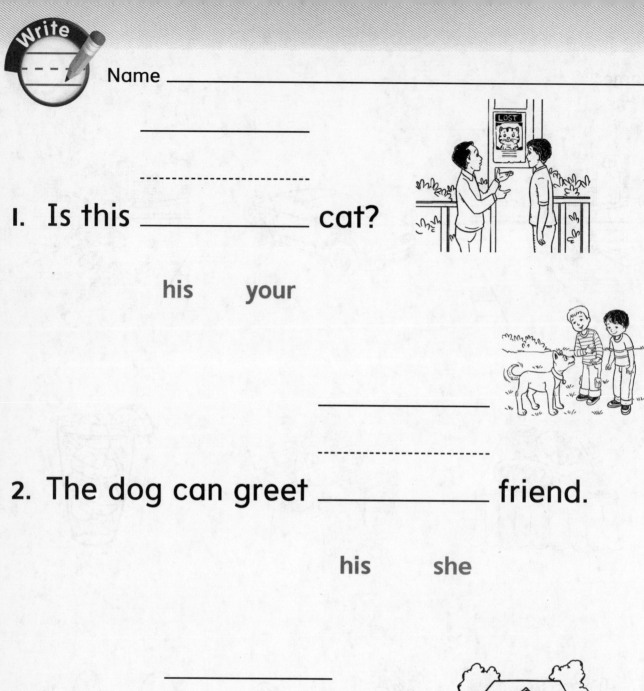

Name _____

_____

‑‑‑‑‑‑‑‑‑‑‑‑‑‑‑‑‑‑‑‑‑

1. Is this _____ cat?

his   your

_____

‑‑‑‑‑‑‑‑‑‑‑‑‑‑‑‑‑‑‑‑‑

2. The dog can greet _____ friend.

his   she

_____

‑‑‑‑‑‑‑‑‑‑‑‑‑‑‑‑‑‑‑‑‑

3. We like _____ home.

him   our

Grammar: Possessive Pronouns

Explain to children that some pronouns tell about what one person or more than one person owns. The pronouns *my, your, her, his, our,* and *their* are pronouns that show what someone or some people own. Write: *My book is funny.* Say: *In that sentence, the pronoun* My *shows who owns the book.* Read each sentence and the two pronouns below it, and identify the picture. Then tell children to complete each sentence with one of the pronouns.

| her | his | my |

_____

1. _____ sink is nice and clean.

_____

2. Steve takes _____ dog to the park.

_____

3. _____ cute dog can do a trick!

Grammar: Possessive Pronouns
Remind children that a possessive pronoun tells about what one or more people own. Read the sentences and point to and name the pictures. Tell children to write a possessive pronoun from the box on the lines to complete each sentence. Then tell children to refer back to a piece of writing that they did during the week and make sure they used pronouns correctly.

Name _____

1. do you see it on the map.

_____

_____

2. We need to take my dog to the vet She does not want to go?

_____

_____

_____

_____

_____

_____

Edit/Proofread

Tell children to listen as you read aloud the sentences. Have them rewrite each sentence so it shows correct capitalization and punctuation. Use gestures to clarify meaning. Then tell children to refer back to a piece of writing they did during the week and check that they used correct capitalization and end punctuation. Tell them to also make sure they used possessive pronouns correctly.

It is good to help!

Can you help, too?

Connect to Community
Encourage children to read the story to a family member or a friend.

We Can Help!

Who can ride a bike?

It does not take gas!

Review High-Frequency Words
Have children set a purpose for reading, such as finding out how everyone can help. Explain that a word is made up of letters. Point to the letter W on page 2. Point out that this is a letter in the word *Where*. Have children point to the letter g in the word *good* on page 4. Model reading from left to right and ask children to demonstrate it. Tell children to point to and say the words *who* and *play*. Model return sweep as well and then have children demonstrate it.

Look! She has a seed.
She can pat the seed in.

Where can they play?
Come and play here!

Name _____

The Alphabet

Aa 	Bb 	Cc 	Dd 	Ee 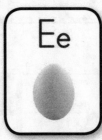	Ff 
Gg 	Hh 	Ii 	Jj 	Kk 	Ll 
Mm 	Nn 	Oo 	Pp 	Qq 	Rr 
Ss 	Tt 	Uu 	Vv 	Ww 	Xx 
Yy 	Zz 				

Handwriting Models

Sound Boxes

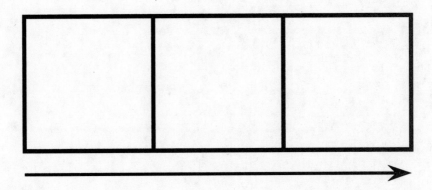

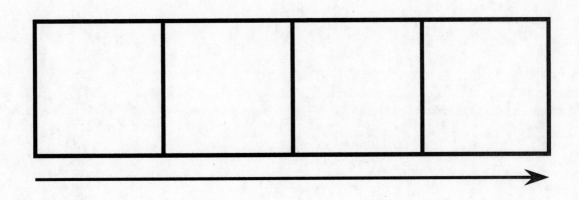

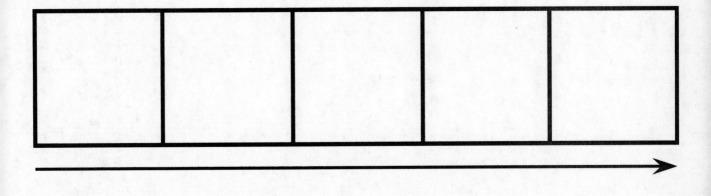

High-Frequency Word Cards

can	we	a
I	the	see

Tim **can** jump.

I can play.

We can see the cat.

We play in **the** sand.

Pam can use **a** ruler.

I can **see** a fish.

High-Frequency Word Cards

to	go	do
like	and	you

Grade K **469**

It is good **to** listen.

Mom and I **go** to the store.

We **do** want to go!

We like pizza!

I see a cat **and** a dog.

Do **you** like milk?

High-Frequency Word Cards

are	with	little
my	he	is

Ted and Ed **are** friends.

I go **with** Ron to the farm.

The bugs are **little**.

Do you like **my** hat?

He ate a red apple.

My bike **is** red.

High-Frequency Word Cards

was	**have**	**of**
she	**for**	**they**

Monday **was** a hot day.

Elephants **have** big ears.

I take care **of** my fish.

She can kick the ball.

This is **for** you.

They went to the park.

474 Grade K

High-Frequency Word Cards

want	me	what
said	here	this

I **want** to see a lion.

The **vet** said Max is fine.

The book **belongs** to me.

The bus is **here**.

What do zebras eat?

I was on **this** street.

476 Grade K

High-Frequency Word Cards

too	has	look
help	play	where

Jake can help, **too**.

My class **has** a pet.

Look at the owl's home.

I **help** to rake the leaves.

Mike and I **play** a game.

Where do roses grow?

High-Frequency Word Cards

good	does	
who	come	

You did a **good** job.

Does this bus go north?

Who can use the paint?

Jake will **come** to my house.

Build Your Word Bank High-Frequency Word Cards

down	jump	our
out	will	there

I walk **down** the hill.

Can a cow **jump** over the moon?

We can use **our** senses.

Jim let the dog **out**.

Tim **will** help me.

Pam lives **there**.

Build Your Word Bank High-Frequency Word Cards

well	one	then
two	her	say

School is going **well** so far.

Sam has **one** map.

Then I went to the store.

I have **two** books.

Her cat is Tam.

I like to **say** please if I need help.

Build Your Word Bank High-Frequency Word Cards

saw

place

all

new

could

white

Kayla **saw** the missing kitten.

I see her **new** hat.

Nat will put the books in the right **place**.

I **could** do that for you.

Mark put **all** the cans in the box.

Tim has **a** **white** cap.

Build Your Word Bank High-Frequency Word Cards

four	long	than
that	day	blue

He has **four** pets.

Pam will use **that** map.

Dan can sing a **long** song.

What **day** of the week is it?

I wrote more **than** Nat.

Dad has a **blue** van.

Build Your Word Bank High-Frequency Word Cards

three	which	many
his	when	soon

Caleb has **three** hats.

Which hen laid the egg?

Bob has **many** pens.

Nan is **his** cat.

I use a pen **when** I write.

We will go home **soon**.

Build Your Word Bank High-Frequency Word Cards

eat	some	now
them	by	brown

We can **eat** popcorn.

Deb will eat **some** snacks.

I can play **now**.

I will ask **them** to play.

Rob sat **by** the fan.

Deb has **brown** hair.

Build Your Word Bank High-Frequency Word Cards

under	how	water
way	from	pretty

The cat hid **under** the bed.

Ben knows the **way** to school.

Kim knows **how** to use the lock.

Kate drinks **from** her cup.

The **water** is hot.

The bug had **pretty** wings.

Build Your Word Bank High-Frequency Word Cards

yellow	work	about
these	people	funny

I have a **yellow** bird.

Nina will **work** hard on her homework.

What is the book **about**?

Please help me move **these** boxes.

Six **people** fit in the van.

It is **funny** when my dog snores.

Build Your Word Bank High-Frequency Word Cards

away	each	
may	or	please

The dog ran **away**.

We will **each** present our projects.

Jack **may** dig a big hole.

Do you like apples **or** oranges?

Please pick up this mess.

Build Your Word Bank High-Frequency Word Cards

into	find	were
other	more	over

Grade K **499**

I can see **into** the cave.

What **other** book do you like?

Can you **find** where she is hiding?

Dave can bake **more** cakes.

Mike and Kate **were** late.

The gull flew **over** the lake.

Build Your Word Bank High-Frequency Word Cards

would	part	words
know	write	only

I hoped my kite **would** fly high.

I want a **part** of the pie.

I **know** the **words** to the song.

I **know** you very well.

Kim will **write** a play.

Dale **only** has one rose.

Build Your Word Bank High-Frequency Word Cards

sound

first

their

I love the **sound** of bells.

You are the **first** one in line.

I know **their** cat.

My Print Concepts Checklist I

☐ Did I identify the front cover of a book?

☐ Did I identify the title page of a book?

☐ Did I identify the back cover of a book?

☐ Can I point to the title of the book?

Print Concepts
Demonstrate the proper way to hold a book, with the front cover facing you and right-side up. Explain to children that a book has a front cover, a back cover, and a title page. Point to each one of these. Then point to the title on the title page and tell children it is the name of the book. Have children choose a book to read and then fill in the checklist on this page.

My Print Concepts Checklist 2

☐ Did I hold my book right-side up?

☐ Can I point to the first word on a page?

☐ Did I read from top to bottom?

☐ Did I read from left to right?

Print Concepts
Model for children how to hold a book right-side up. Point to the first word on a page and demonstrate reading a page from top to bottom and left to right. Tell children that when they get to the end of a line they should go to the start of the next line. Have children choose a book to read and have them demonstrate these print awareness skills. After reading, have them fill in the checklist on this page.

My Print Concepts Checklist 3

☐ Can I point to the first word on a page?

☐ Did I read from top to bottom?

☐ Did I read from left to right?

☐ Did I know where to read when I got to the end of the line?

Print Concepts
Remind children that they need to read from left to right and from the top to the bottom of a page. Explain that when they get to the end of a line they should go to the start of the next line and continue reading. Model these print concepts for children. Then have children choose a book to read and fill out the checklist on this page.

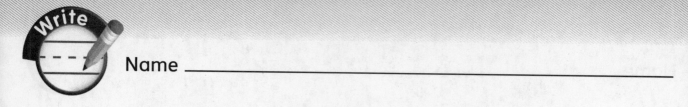

Name _____

My Print Concepts Checklist 4

☐ Did I know where to read when I got to the end of a line?

☐ Can I point to the first word in a sentence?

☐ Can I point to the last word in a sentence?

☐ Can I count the words in a sentence?

Print Concepts

Remind children that when they get to the end of a line, they need to continue reading on the next line. Point out that there is a space between each word in a sentence. Model pointing to the space between words and then how to count the number of words in a sentence. Also remind children that sentences can end with a period, a question mark, or an exclamation mark. Model these print concepts for children. Then have children choose a book to read and fill out the checklist on this page.

My Print Concepts Checklist 5

☐   **Did I identify the title page of a book?**

☐   **Did I know where to read when I got to the end of a line?**

☐   **Can I point to a letter in a word?**

☐   **Can I point to the first and last words in a sentence?**

Print Concepts
Remind children that a book has a front cover, a title page, and a back cover. Tell them to hold the book correctly and to turn the pages of the book from right to left. Remind them that when they get to the end of a line, they need to continue reading on the next line. Point out the difference between the letter *b* and the word *book*. Model these print concepts for children. Then have children choose a book to read and fill out the checklist on this page.

My Print Concepts Checklist 5

Did I identify the title page of a book?

Did I know where to read when I got to the end of a line?

Can I point to a letter in a word?

Can I point to the first and last words in a sentence?

Name _____

Phonics Review Game: /m/m, /a/a, /s/s, /p/p, /t/t
Say the name of each item and the letter it begins with. Turn the picture over and trace the letters. With a partner, think of other things whose names begin with each sound and letter.

t	m	a	s
s	p	s	m
m	p	t	a

Phonics Review Game: /m/m, /a/a, /s/s, /p/p, /t/t
Trace the letters. Say each letter and its sound. Then name a word that begins with the letter.

Phonics Review Game: /i/i, /n/n, /k/c, /o/o, /d/d
Say the name of each item and the letter it begins with. Then cut out each picture.

Phonics Review Game: */i/i, /n/n, /k/c, /o/o, /d/d*
Place the picture cards face-down onto a desk or table. Flip two cards over and say the names of the pictures. Have children say the letter that stands for each beginning sound. If the pictures begin with the same letter, you have made a match. Continue playing until all cards have been matched.

Name _____

End

Start

Phonics Review Game: /h/h, /e/e, /f/f, /r/r, /b/b, /l/l

Place a marker on "Start." Move your marker from square to square. When you land on a picture, say the name of the picture and the letter it begins with. If you land on a letter, say a word that begins with that letter. You may also wish to distribute cards with the numbers 1, 2, and 3 for children to use to move however many spaces the card says. When you reach "End," play again and think of new words.

Name _____

b   ck

Phonics Review Game: /b/b, /k/ck
Say the name of each picture. Draw lines to connect the pictures to the letters they end with. Work with a partner to think of other words that end with each of these sounds. Then use the words in sentences.

516   Grade K • Unit 6 • Week 3

Name _____

End

Start

Phonics Review Game: /u/u, /g/g, /w/w, /v/v, /j/j, /kw/qu, /y/y, /z/z

Place a marker on "Start." Move your marker from square to square. When you land on a picture, say the name of the picture and the letter it begins with. If you land on a letter, say a word that begins with that letter. You may also wish to distribute 3 cards with a number on each one. When you reach "End," play again and think of new words.

Grade K • Unit 8 • Week 3   **517**

   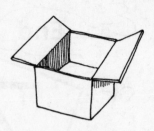

g   x

Phonics Review Game: /g/g, /ks/x
Say the name of each picture. Draw lines to connect the pictures to the letters they end with. Encourage pairs of children to think of other words that end with these sounds. Tell them to work with a partner and use the words in sentences.

Phonics Review Game: /ā/a_e, /ī/i_e, /ō/o_e, /ū/u_e, /ē/e, ee
Cut on the dotted lines. Fold on the solid lines and tape together to make a cube.

Name _____

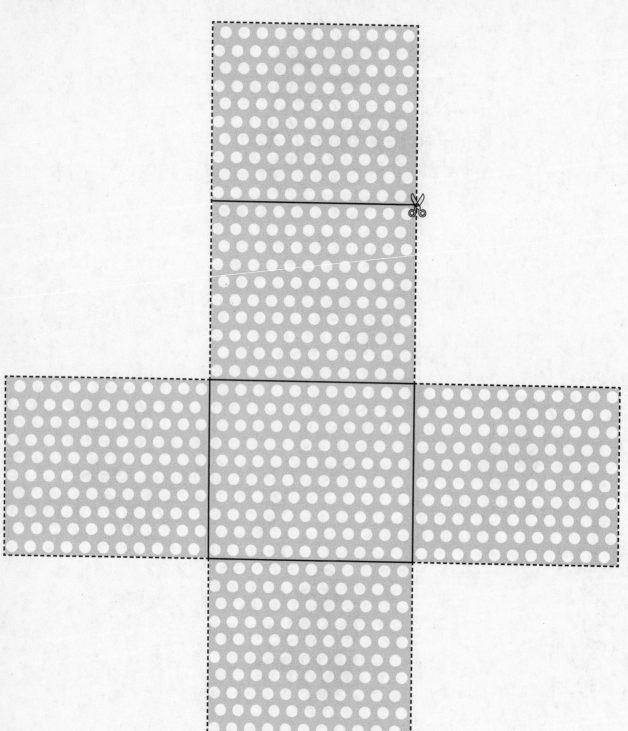

Phonics Review Game: /ā/a_e, / ī/i_e, /ō/o_e, /ū/u_e, /ē/e, ee
Toss the cube with a partner. Say the name of the picture that faces up. Say the long vowel sound you hear in the word. Then say another word that has that long vowel sound.

My Strategies and Tools

Student-Centered Learning

As children begin to learn the skills and strategies that help them think critically as they read, write, and participate in discussions and group projects, it is important to give them independent opportunities to apply what they learn.

How to Use the Blackline Masters:

1. Provide a blackline master to children and review with them as you explicitly teach the corresponding lesson.

Listen Carefully	Start Smart, Week I, SI3
Ask Questions	Unit I, Week I, T8
Character	Unit I, Week I, T8
Retell a Text	Unit I, Week I, TI3
Respond to a Text	Unit I, Week I, TI3
Make a Connection	Unit I, Week I, T33
Research Plan	Unit I, Week I, T54
Choose a Book	Unit I, Week I, T7I
Who Is Telling the Story?	Unit 4, Week 2, T374
Combine Information	Unit 4, Week 3, T42I
Make Inferences	Unit 6, Week 3, T42I
Make a Prediction	Unit 7, Week 2, T86
Check Your Prediction	Unit 7, Week 2, T86

2. After teaching the lesson, ask children to discuss the blackline master during small group independent time.

3. Display the blackline masters in the reading center. As you assign independent work, direct children's attention to a specific blackline master to review.

Listen Carefully

Listen with your **WHOLE BODY!**

eyes watching

brain thinking

mouth quiet

ears listening

heart caring

body facing the speaker

hands still

feet still

Ask Questions

Asking questions can help you understand
what you read.

Before

Ask about

- the title, art, or photos.
- what you will find out.
- what you want to understand.

During

Ask about

- ideas you do not understand.
- words you do not know.
- the characters in a story.
- an event from a text.

After

Ask about

- something you still want
  to understand.
- more information you
  want to know.

The characters are the people or animals a made-up story is about. Find details about the characters in the text, pictures, or photos.

Jim has a dog.

The dog's name is Spot.

Spot is white with black spots.

Jim and Spot like to run.

They have fun together.

Details About The Dog

The dog's name is Spot.

Spot is white with black spots.

Read a text with a partner.
Talk about the characters.
Identify details about the characters.

Retell a Text

When you retell a text, you tell the important details.

1. Look at the pictures on each page.

2. Tell your partner the important details in order.

3. Take turns with your partner.

Respond to a Text

Share what you learn about a text. Use text evidence in your response. Make a connection to the text. Use new words you learned.

Talk About It

- Talk to a partner.
- Discuss the topic. Talk about what the text is about.
- Tell how you connected to the text.

Write About It

- Write complete sentences.
- Read your writing.

Draw a Picture

- Write labels.
- Talk about your picture.

Make a connection to what you read.
Share your connection with a partner.

This connects to a time when I ...

This connects to another book I read because ...

This connects to my world because ...

Research Plan

Follow the steps.

Step 1
Choose a topic.
- What do you want to find out about?

Step 2
Write your questions.
- What do you want to learn?

Step 3
Decide where to find the answers.
- Talk to an expert or read a text.
- Find the information you need.

Step 4
Write what you learn.
- Draw pictures.
- Write the answers to your questions.

Step 5
Choose how to present your work.

Write about it!   Create a model.

Do a demonstration.

 Share what you learned!

How to choose a book:

- Pick a book. Open it to any page.
- Read all the words on the page.
- Put one finger up for each word you can't figure out.

Five Finger Rule

0 – 1 Finger	This book will be easy for you. Make sure you don't choose too many books that are too easy for you.
2 – 3 Fingers	This is a great choice!
4 Fingers	Give this book a try.
5 Fingers	This is a challenging book. You might want to make another choice.

Now spend time reading. Try to read a little longer each time.

Who Is Telling the Story?

Listen to the story. Talk about who is telling the story. Is it a character who tells the story or a narrator who tells the story?

Character telling the story

Look for the words **I, me,** and **my.**

I saw my mom.

Character

Narrator telling the story

Look for the words **he, she, they,** and **characters' names.**

They saw a bird.

Narrator

Combine Information

Each page of a text gives you information. The information on every page is connected. Sometimes new information can change what you understand about a text.

= What I Learned

- **Read a page.**
  Tell a partner what you learned.

- **Read another page.**
  Tell a partner what you learned.
  Did your understanding of the text change?

- **Tell how the information is connected.**
  Take turns with your partner.

Make Inferences

Sometimes an author does not tell you some information.

- Think about clues in the text or pictures.
- Think about what you already know.
- Put the clues and what you know together.
- Make an inference.

The text tells me ...
And I know that ...
So I think ...

Make a Prediction

A prediction is a guess about what will happen next. To make a prediction, you can use information from the text.

> ## Text Features
>
> Look at the photos and illustrations.
> Look at the captions.
> What information will you learn?

> ## Text Structure
>
> Talk about how the text is organized.
> What happened first?
> What may happen next?

Check Your Prediction

Check to see if your predictions are correct. If they are not correct, you can always change them.

Text Features

Look at the photos and illustrations.

Look at the captions.

What information did you learn?

Text Structure

Think about how the text is organized.

What happened?

Name

My Notes

Name _____

My Notes